Oswald
Chambers

WOMEN OF FAITH SERIES

MEN OF FAITH SERIES

WOMEN AND MEN OF FAITH

OTHER BIOGRAPHIES FROM BETHANY HOUSE

Oswald Chambers

David W. Lambert

BETHANY HOUSE PUBLISHERS
MINNEAPOLIS, MINNESOTA 55438

Oswald Chambers
Copyright © 1997
David W. Lambert

Reprinted 1972, 1979, 1981; the first American edition 1983
Christian Literature Crusade
Fort Washington, Pennsylvania 19034
Published under special arrangement with the Oswald Chambers
Publications Association, Limited, U.K.

Published by Bethany House Publishers
A Ministry of Bethany Fellowship International
11400 Hampshire Avenue South
Minneapolis, Minnesota 55438
www.bethanyhouse.com

Printed in the United States of America by
Bethany Press International, Minneapolis, Minnesota 55438

Library of Congress Catalog Card Number 97–4646

ISBN 1–55661–942–1

We cannot kindle when we will
The fire which in the heart resides;
The spirit bloweth and is still,
In mystery our soul abides.
But tasks in hours of insight will'd
Can be through hours of gloom fulfilled.
With aching hands and bleeding feet,
We dig and heap, lay stones on stone;
We bear the burden and the heat
Of the long day and wish were done.
Not till the light return,
All we have built do we discern.

—Matthew Arnold, *Morality*

Contents

Introduction by Jim Reimann

As the editor of the updated edition of *My Utmost for His Highest*, I often hear people say: "It's as if my name were at the top of today's devotional—the message was exactly what I needed to hear and spoke directly to my heart." Many people think of this occurrence as something mystical or magical in nature, and wonder why the devotionals speak to them day after day and year after year. Yet my answer is that there is nothing unusual happening to them at all, but that Oswald Chambers had a way of quickly cutting through all the mundane issues of life and getting to the heart of the matter. In his teachings he did not talk about the weather, sports, or other temporal things, but daily brought his listeners face-to-face with Jesus Christ and their relationship with Him. When we read Chambers' writings we are confronted with the truth of Christ, which causes us to examine our own hearts. Then, if we are open to the Lord, He can use His Word to comfort and encourage us, or to bring about change in our lives.

Chambers was a master at communicating a profound truth in a simple and understandable way. His preaching and teaching was akin to that of the apostle Paul who said, "I resolved to know nothing while I was with you except Jesus Christ and him crucified. My message and my preaching were not with wise and persuasive words, but with a demonstration of the Spirit's power, so that your faith might not rest on men's wisdom, but on God's power" (1 Corinthians 2:2, 4–5).

My Utmost for His Highest and the other writings of Oswald Chambers became a part of my daily devotional life when I was twenty-three. As a relatively new Christian, his books became a tremendous resource to ground me in the biblical doctrines of the faith, for his teachings have always pointed me to Jesus Christ and His powerful Word. And still today when I hear certain concepts, such as God engineering our circumstances, abandoning ourselves to Christ, or our lives being broken bread or poured-out wine for the Lord, I think of the teachings of Chambers.

Some years ago, the Lord led me to create an updated edition of *My Utmost for His Highest*. I had been a Christian retailer for many years at the time and had sold thousands of copies of the original edition. For some time, however, I had heard many believers express their inability to fully understand what they were reading. It was not so much that Chambers' thoughts were difficult to comprehend, but that the English language had changed considerably since his words were first put to paper. And many of the "British-isms" he used only added to the American readers' lack of understanding. My concern was that his great teachings would be lost for many people in this generation, not to mention the generations to come.

As I began work on the new edition of *My Utmost*, I found myself wanting to know more about the man behind the words. One of the few books I was able to find on Chambers' life was a little book entitled *An Unbribed Soul*. The book you now hold in your hands is a revision of that concise biography and has been retitled *Oswald Chambers*, as a part of Bethany House Publishers' MEN OF FAITH series. It was in this little book that I learned that Chambers died at the early age of forty-three.

As I have shared this fact with others, many have said, "What a shame Chambers died such an untimely death!" I feel certain Chambers would have loved to continue preaching and ministering to others, but because of his strong belief in the sovereignty of God, I doubt he would agree his death was untimely. As he often said, "God engineers our circumstances," and I am sure he would have taken that to mean even the circumstances of his own death. I personally believe his books have probably reached a wider audience over time as a result, not in spite of, his so-called "untimely" death.

Upon the republication of this biography, Oswald Chambers will have been dead for eighty years. Yet his words live on, and he is more widely known today than ever before. Literally millions of people around the world have been introduced to him through his writings, especially *My Utmost for His Highest*, which was compiled by Chambers' wife after his death. And although many people may know his books, few know the story of the man behind them. And few people know the story of how God used Mrs. Chambers for nearly fifty years after Oswald's death to sacrificially print and distribute his teachings throughout the world.

This biography, first published more than twenty-five years ago, was written by David W. Lambert, whose father was a friend of Oswald Chambers. It will give you a glimpse into the man behind the books that have become like dear friends to so many of us. You will learn that God sovereignly brought to Chambers a wife who "just happened" to be a court stenographer, and who "just happened" to write down all of his teachings verbatim. And you will see how God worked in his life and circumstances to fashion him into the vessel the Lord has used to speak to untold millions of people through the printed page for many years beyond his death.

Perhaps this book will also help you to see a very humble and human side of Oswald Chambers. As I have learned more about him over the last several years, I have come to realize that many of us have had preconceived and factually incorrect ideas about what he must have been like. In fact, the wife of the principal of the Bible Training Center, where Chambers had been a student, described him this way, shortly after his death:

> How can Oswald Chambers be condensed into anything like a readable reminiscence? He was not one man, but many men. There is no label that one can attach to him and be satisfied—artist, poet, philosopher, preacher and teacher, comedian—for he had a delicious sense of humor and dramatic power, if he cared to use it.

Yes, Oswald Chambers was a multi-faceted man, but first and foremost, one who had a deep and abiding relationship with his Lord Jesus Christ. I trust this little book will not only give you a better understanding of the life of Chambers but also help you to see what God can do with a life that is totally abandoned to Him.

—James Reimann, Editor,
My Utmost for His Highest,
   updated edition;
Streams in the Desert,
   updated edition

Preface

It was 1915, during the time of the Great War. A tall athletic figure was standing in the kitchen of the cottage in the Yorkshire Dales. He had come to say goodbye. "I am going out to Egypt to help the men in the armed forces. I have a text: 'I am ready to be offered' (2 Timothy 4). I do not know what it means, but I am ready."

I was only in my teens, but that scene has forever remained with me. Oswald Chambers was a friend of my father and had indeed been a great spiritual help to him, and now these final days of summer holiday were spent together. The greatness of the man came out in the simplicity and gaiety of his life on holiday.

Then there were the days when he stayed in our home. Unlike some earnest guest preachers, he did not probe the younger members of the family concerning their spiritual state. He just treated us normally and entered into our boyish interests. How well I remember him one day after lunch sitting on a couch and picking up a copy of the *Boys Own Annual* and saying, "I am going to study this tome of theology." No, he never spoke to me about my soul, but his life in the home made an impression that created a hunger after reality.

Many memories come back of his joyful life. On one occasion when my mother was preparing the tea, to which a number of local ministers had been invited to meet Chambers, there came gales of laughter from the study. I, with the priggishness of a small boy, looked shocked, thinking that such holy men should not indulge in laughter. My mother, with quiet insight, remarked, "When God makes you holy, He gives you a sense of humor."

Then came the time when Chambers' books became part of my life, and more and more I found in them the answer to so many spiritual and practical problems.

Now there comes the urge to write a brief study of the one who has meant so much to so many through the years. Oswald Chambers would have deprecated any attempt to exalt either the man or his teaching into a cult, and that is not our purpose.

It is rather to set out for the benefit of a new generation, to whom Oswald Chambers is but a name, the facts of his life and the amazing ministry that followed his home call at the early age of forty-three. The biography *Life*, compiled by Mrs. Chambers, is still available and we have drawn much upon it. We trust that this smaller book will introduce people again to that remarkable biography so full of firsthand tributes from those who knew the man and valued his message.

We are most grateful to Kathleen Chambers for all her help and encouragement and for material hitherto unused that she has put into our hands. I would also pay tribute to my father, Rev. David Lambert, who through the years helped Mrs. Chambers in producing the books, and left behind valuable notes and comments on the message of this man of God.

Finally, my grateful thanks are due to Marie Goring, for her generous and efficient help with the manuscript.

—David W. Lambert

Prologue

The influence of Oswald Chambers is stronger than ever today. Thousands of people have read his books, although these have had little publicity through the years. Ministers of various churches and missionaries of different societies find continual inspiration from his writings, and most of all from that remarkable book of daily readings, *My Utmost for His Highest*, now recognized as a spiritual classic.

The interest is not confined to evangelical circles. Brother Douglas, of the Anglican Franciscans, who had known Chambers in Egypt, treasured his books; in his biography we are told that this saint of God kept a copy of *My Utmost* at his bedside and meditated on it literally to his dying days.

Recently, the Archbishop of York, Dr. Coggan, in his lectures on preaching ("Stewards of Grace"), quoted at length from Oswald Chambers; while the Dean of Westminster, Dr. Eric Abbott, included Oswald Chambers in a course of Lenten lectures on "Some Masters of the Spiritual Life," bracketing him with Lancelot Andrews, John Bunyan, and Von Hugel.

Yet another modern divine, J. E. Fison (now

Bishop of Salisbury), wrote a penetrating study of Chambers as an evangelical prophet in the journal *Theology* (see Appendix A).

Indeed, the influence of this man of God is found working like leaven in many quiet and unexpected places. Thus in a country church in the lake district we found a copy of *My Utmost for His Highest* in the pulpit, the vicar telling us that he fed his soul on the writings of Chambers and ranked him with Blaise Pascal and George MacDonald.

What is the explanation of this abiding influence? We hope this book will give some clue. The answer we feel is in the man and the message and the two are inextricably bound together.

We believe we are right in saying that Oswald Chambers himself wrote no books. All that has been published during the years began with an inspiration to share with the men in Egypt, to whom he had ministered something of his abiding message. This is a story to be told later (see Epilogue).

THE MAN

1

A Vessel Prepared

David Brainerd, pioneer missionary to the Indians of South America, died at the age of twenty-nine; Robert Murray McCheyne, the saintly Scottish preacher, at thirty; and Henry Martyn at thirty-one. Looking back, one senses a completeness in these comparatively short lives. "Having lived a short time, they fulfilled a long time."

So it was with Oswald Chambers, whose life was "cut short," as men would say, at the age of forty-three, when he seemed to be at the height of his powers. Looking back now over fifty years, there is again a sense of divine completion. Moreover, the years that have elapsed since have seen a harvest, through the spreading abroad of his message, such as could hardly have been had he lived on.

Dr. Rattenbury, writing of John Wesley's transforming experience in May 1738, said, "The flame fell on a well-laid fire." The years of home discipline in the Epworth rectory, the care of a godly mother, the Holy Club at Oxford with its ordered and sacrificial life—these made up the well-laid fire on which, in the upper room at Aldersgate Street, the flame of God fell with such abiding effect.

So with Chambers the tremendous and shattering experience that made him into God's flaming prophet had a background of some thirty years' preparation.

First and foremost, a godly home. Oswald's father was a Baptist minister and was baptized himself under Charles Haddon Spurgeon, along with his wife, who had formerly belonged to the Catholic Apostolic Church, founded by Edward Irving. When Oswald was born on July 24, 1874, his father was minister at Crown Terrace Baptist Church, Aberdeen. Later the family moved first to Stoke-on-Trent for two years, and then to Perth for eight years. During this time Oswald developed both physically and mentally, climbing Kinnoul Hill and exploring the banks of the Tay. The next move was to Southgate, London. Here Oswald's love for art developed and for some time seems to have possessed his thoughts and his ambition. After studying at the Kensington Art School, he won a scholarship and might have traveled for two years on the Continent. He refused this offer, for he had seen other students come back as moral and physical wrecks. Meanwhile, he had undergone an evangelical conversion. He and his father were on their way home from a service conducted by Spurgeon, when Oswald remarked that had there been an opportunity he would have given his life to Christ. His father replied, "You can do it now, my boy," and there and then, standing under a gas lamp in the street, he took Christ as his Savior. Shortly afterward, he was baptized and joined Rye Lane Baptist Church where the family had become members.

The influence of his mother during these vital days is revealed in a letter that he wrote when he was thirty, and about to sail for Japan:

My dear "brick" of a Mother,

I am proud of your letter, and more than proud of such a mother. . . . God has undertaken mightily. The enervation caused by the fondness and attachment of home folks has so often been terrible in an outgoing missionary's life. If it is possible, I love you more than ever for being so robust and strong in your mind. Thank God for you and upon every remembrance of you. God surely has wonderfully answered your prayers for your children. The memory of Mother's doings and managings are to me a growing stimulus and an amazement, while her detestation of can't and humbug also seems to have left in me no little of the same spirit. I, as your youngest son, see you both transfigured in the light of years and life. I thank God for you, and praise Him that neither of you ever offered any obstacle to my following what appeared to me God's calls, for the ways and turnings have perplexed you much; but, thank God, He has allowed you to live to see that when He leads all is well.

Ever your loving son,
Oswald

Another formative influence was that of Christian service. Oswald became intimate with a group of earnest young people attached to the church, and soon he was sharing with them in Sunday school teaching and in evangelistic outreach, visiting lodging houses, etc. He attended weekly prayer meetings regularly, but for some time did not take any vocal part. Then he broke through, and his prayers were unusual. Someone remembers him praying, "Lord, drench us with humility," a remarkable prayer for one so young in the faith.

There seems to have been a rapid development in

real spiritual understanding. This is evident in a paper that he sent to be read at a worker's conference at the Relf Road Mission. The theme was "Holy Patience":

Probably *the* charm in a Christian that appeals to others most beseechingly, winning their hearts from sordidness, their souls from despondency, and their tongues from speaking guile, is the charm of holy patience. These holy ones have about them the unconscious influence and power of Jesus Christ on whom their minds ever dwell, to whom their souls breathe constant prayer, for whom they toil unceasingly. These live a noble life because it is deep, and knowing enough of themselves they are not unduly concerned about themselves. By that holy patience would we be possessed. Those who have attained to holy patience are like the nightingale singing through the night; they endure as seeing Him who is invisible.

Another landmark was the day when he left home to take an arts course at Edinburgh. He was to miss the home that had meant so much through the years, but there was a thrill in returning to Scotland. So he wrote in his diary:

Edinburgh, Scotland, all hail! How my soul beats and strains and yearns for you; Scotland, bonnie, bonnie Scotland, how I love you! It'll not be long now afore I'll be amang yir hills and braes and woods, Scotland. Ye'll give me the steadfastness of yir everlasting hills, the strength of yir storm-torn firs, the power of yir mountain streams, the tenderness of yir bluebells, and the faithfulness of yir noble pride.

God is the mover, prime and sole, above and

through circumstances. I feel traits in my character I knew not of before and it causes me to bow in deeper gratitude for that home training, which I have now left for the training and discipline of life. Oh, what a mighty influence homelife has on us! Indeed, we do not know how deep a debt we owe to our mothers and fathers and their training.

His lodgings in Livingstone Place had just been vacated by J. H. Jowett, later to become perhaps the greatest preacher of his day, and Oswald felt he was in a noble succession.

According to the University records, Oswald Chambers matriculated in 1895, enrolling for the Arts course, his name appearing in the class list for Classical Archaeology.

Already we see his strong artistic temperament emerging, but with a Christian element coming to the fore. Thus he writes: "My life work as I see it . . . is to strike for the redemption of the aesthetic kingdom—music and art and poetry—or rather the proving of Christ's redemption of it."

The service of art even for Christ's sake was soon to be surrendered in answer to a yet higher call. To this we must now turn.

2

The Call—Heard and Obeyed

We are apt to forget the mystic supernatural touch of God that comes with His call. If a man can tell you how he got the call of God and all about it, it is questionable whether he ever had the call. A call to be a professional man may come in that explicit way, but the call of God is much more supernatural. The realization of the call of God in a man's life may come as a sudden thunderclap or by a gradual dawning, but in whatever way it comes, it comes with the undercurrent of the supernatural, almost the uncanny, and it is always accompanied with a glow—something that cannot be put into words. We need to keep the atmosphere of our mind prepared by the Holy Spirit lest we forget the surprise of the touch of God on our lives.

> —from Chambers' book *So Send I You*

During the time in Edinburgh, Oswald Chambers was increasingly aware of the call of God. His deep sensitive nature was greatly stirred, and he was especially concerned about the lack of Christian witness in the realm of art (he was studying Fine Art and Archaeology at the time). He writes to a friend:

> Art seems settling to the sensually reposeful position of previous ages. . . . The Spirit of God seems to cry, "Whom shall I send and who will go for us?" Then through all my weaknesses, my sinfulness, and my frailties my soul cries, "Here am I, send me." I do not know how it is to be done; but if God calls, He will guide, I know, and we shall one day see the travail of the soul of Christ satisfied and all the kingdoms of this world laid at His feet.

There was much struggle of soul, and slowly but surely the impression developed that art was to be left and the call to the ministry accepted. The decision was not easily reached, and something of what it cost him and indeed the soul travail that he went through is revealed in the following excerpt of a letter written to a very dear friend when Chambers was about twenty years of age:

> The emotion that is strongest is that of entering the ministry; how often I have hinted at it and how often stifled it back down. I must not, for I cannot, keep it hid any longer, and it is perplexing me tremendously. It would be playing with the sacred touch of God to neglect or stifle again this strange yet deep conviction, that sometime I must be a minister. My inward conviction—the decided thwarting of the practical art line—nay, the repeated and pointed shutting of doors that seemed just opening, and the confident opinion of friends, lead me to consider most earnestly before God what His will is. . . . I am going to leave the opening of the way to the ministry in His hands. . . . Brighter, clearer, and more exquisite is the spir-

itual becoming within, and oh, my whole being is ablaze and passionately on fire to preach Christ; my art aim is swallowed up in this now. . . . By the grace of God, when the way is clear I'll go—obstruct who may, laugh who will, scoff who can. . . . I am completely perplexed and hemmed in on every side, but the joy that is sometimes eloquent within me is so great that it overwhelms me with gratitude. I feel I am in the mighty hands of God, and that if I am patient the issue will be in accordance with His will.

In the midst of this overwhelming spiritual experience, Chambers was not unaware of the practical situation in which he found himself. Students in those days did not receive grants, and the economic pressure was at times severe. Yet even of this he could write in the spirit of quiet faith:

For three weeks now I have had no work—art, portrait paintings, all my commissions are finished and I have no new ones. I have not been able to pay my landlady for some time and I have, as my sole money possession in this world 1/8d. . . . This coming week brings no shadow of a prospect. I look at home and see a great need there, and yet I have tried and prayed to gain money sufficient to help them. I am not afraid; I am not downcast; I am serious, fervently serious, that I can face the whole unflinchingly because my faith and consolation is in the Lord my God. . . . I have been through worse times with only 6d. in my pocket, and all has been well because God was there. It will all be all right; never let my home folks know anything about this. . . . I am not in the least disturbed about these hard times; night and day my soul is yearning and crying and my spirit waiting

for a great absorbing work to come for me to en-
gage in for His sake; we will look up and be strong
and of a good courage. God is not very far off.

In spite of circumstances, there was the assur-
ance of God's plan. The very failure of opportunity
in the realm of art seemed to underline the call that
was pressing upon him.

It must have been just at this time, while spend-
ing a night in prayer on Arthur's Seat, above the
city of Edinburgh, the young student was conscious
of a voice saying to him, "I need you for My service,
but I can do without you." The choice was made and
there could now be no going back. Oswald Chambers returned to his lodgings to find awaiting him
an envelope containing the prospectus of Dunoon
College. This was God's answer.

3

The Crisis—The Refining Fire

Dunoon College was a small independent training center for young men hoping to enter the Baptist ministry.[1] The principal, Dr. MacGregor, was a remarkable character, scholarly and spiritual. No doubt the young university student was an unusual candidate. This is suggested by the fact that after a short time in residence Chambers became a student tutor. He taught Logic, Moral Philosophy, and Psychology, actually preparing a book entitled *Outlines for the Study of Historical Philosophy*, based on his lectures; these were often illustrated by diagrams. He worked hard, getting up at six and filling the day with strenuous activity. The habits of those early days remained through the years. (We well remember his saying on one occasion, "I would rather have the devil in my study than an armchair.") Apart from his college work he did some art teaching and wrote articles on literary and artistic themes. He also started a Browning society and introduced his favorite poet both to students and

---

[1]Now Dhalling Mhor Guest House.

townsfolk. He became an active member of the Dunoon Baptist Church, leading the Christian Endeavor and a young people's class. He loved music and played classical pieces to the joy of others of like tastes.

Perhaps this period in his life is best described by Mrs. MacGregor, writing after his home call:

> How can Oswald Chambers be condensed into anything like a readable reminiscence? He was not one man but many men. There is no label that one can attach to him and be satisfied—artist, poet, philosopher, preacher and teacher, comedian—for he had a delicious sense of humor and dramatic power, if he cared to use it. Two of his sayings especially remain with me: "I refuse to worry," with a very marked emphasis on "refuse." The other was "Wherefore judge nothing before the time, until the Lord come." Refusing to worry, he also refused to criticize, and it would be well if we could all take that stand.

His recreation was mainly walking, and he loved to tramp the Scottish hills with some of the fine characters he met among the Highland people, with whom he found so much in common. During these years at Dunoon, of which most would feel that Chambers had reached the goal of effective service and Christian maturity, there came a remarkable and indeed shattering experience. This we feel is so vital that we can only give in full the record as he himself gave it when speaking some years later in Exeter Hall:

> After I was "born again" as a lad, I enjoyed the presence of Jesus Christ wonderfully, but years

passed before I gave myself up thoroughly to His work.

I was in Dunoon College as tutor of philosophy when Dr. F. B. Meyer came and spoke about the Holy Spirit. I determined to have all that was going and went to my room and asked God simply and definitely for the baptism of the Holy Spirit, whatever that meant. From that day on, for four years, nothing but the overruling grace of God and the kindness of friends kept me out of an asylum. God used me during those years for the conversion of souls, but I had no conscious communion with Him. The Bible was the dullest, most uninteresting book in existence, and the sense of depravity, the vileness, and bad-motivedness of my nature was terrific.

I see now that God was taking me by the light of the Holy Spirit and His Word through every ramification of my being. The last three months of those years things reached a climax; I was getting very desperate. I knew no one who had what I wanted; in fact, I did not know what I did want. But I knew that if what I had was all the Christianity there was, the thing was a fraud. Then Luke 11:13 got hold of me: "If ye then, being evil, know how to give good gifts unto your children: how much more shall your heavenly Father give the Holy Spirit to them that ask him?" But how could I, bad-motived as I was, possibly ask for the gift of the Holy Spirit? Then it was borne in upon me that I had to claim the gift from God on the authority of Jesus Christ and testify to having done so. But the thought came: *If you claim the gift of the Holy Spirit on the word of Jesus Christ and testify to it, God will make it known to those who know you best how bad you are in heart.* And I was not willing to be a fool for Christ's sake. But those of you who know the experience, know very well how God brings one to the point of utter despair, and I got to the place where I did not care whether everyone knew how bad I was; I cared for nothing on earth, save to get out of my present condition.

At a little meeting held during a missions conference in Dunoon, a well-known lady was asked to take the after-meeting. She did not speak, but set us to prayer, and then sang "Touch Me Again, Lord." I felt nothing, but I knew emphatically my time had come, and I rose to my feet. I had no vision of God, only a sheer dogged determination to take God at His Word and to prove this thing for myself, and I stood up and said so. That was bad enough, but what followed was ten times worse. After I had sat down, the speaker, who knew me well, said, "That is very good of our brother; he has spoken like that as an example to the rest of you." Up I got again and said, "I got up for no one's sake; I got up for my own sake; either Christianity is a downright fraud, or I have not got hold of the right end of the stick." And then and there I claimed the gift of the Holy Spirit in dogged committal on Luke 11:13. I had no vision of heaven or of angels; I had nothing. I was as dry and empty as ever—no power or realization of God, no witness of the Holy Spirit. Later I was asked to speak at a meeting, and forty souls came forward. Did I praise God? No, I was terrified and left them to the workers, and went to Mr. MacGregor and told him what had happened. He said, "Don't you remember claiming the Holy Spirit as a gift on the word of Jesus, and that He said, 'Ye shall receive power. . . .'? This is the power from on high." And like a flash, something happened inside me, and I saw that I had been wanting power in my own hand, so to speak, that I might say, "Look what I have got by putting my all on the altar."

If the previous years had been hell on earth, these four years have truly been heaven on earth. Glory be to God, the last aching abyss of the human heart is filled to overflowing with the love of God. Love is the beginning, love is the middle, and love is the end. After He comes in, all you see is "Jesus only, Jesus ever." When you know what God has done for you, the power and the tyranny of sin is gone, and the radiant, unspeakable emancipation of the indwelling Christ is come. When you see men and women who should be princes and princesses with God bound up in a show of things—oh, you begin to understand what the apostle meant when he said he wished that he himself were accursed from Christ that men might be saved.

Just as John Wesley's friends could not understand his Aldersgate experience, so to many this experience of Oswald Chambers—in some ways similar to Wesley's—presents a problem. How is it to be defined? Can it be explained? So far as we know, Chambers rarely referred to it directly. Yet, in a sense, the remaining years of his life are a commentary upon it and the key to it. The mystics used to speak of "the dark night of the soul," a time of spiritual darkness and dryness; not the direct result of sins committed, but rather a deep conviction of sin itself within the heart and mind. To use a phrase Chambers himself often used, "he was being brought to an end of himself," and made aware of the utter worthlessness of his own nature when stripped of all pietistic pretensions. Moreover, there was the willingness to abandon all for

Christ's sake, to deny—as William Penn, the
Quaker, put it—not only his evil self but his good
self. What this must have cost him is suggested by
a paragraph in the booklet *Discipline of Loneliness*:

> Alone! Relinquish all! You cannot consecrate
> your children, your wife, your lover, your friend,
> your father, your mother, or your own life as
> yours. You must abandon all and fling yourself on
> God as a mere conscious being and, unperplexed,
> seeking you will find Him. The teaching that
> presents consecration as giving to God our gifts,
> our possessions, our comrades, is a profound er-
> ror. These are all abandoned, and we give up for-
> ever our right to ourselves. A sanctified soul may
> be an artist, or a musician, but he is not a sanc-
> tified artist or musician. He is one who expresses
> the message of God through a particular medium.
> As long as the artist or musician imagines he can
> consecrate his artistic gifts to God, he is deluded.
> Abandonment of ourselves is the seed of conse-
> cration—not presenting our gifts, but presenting
> ourselves without reserve.

No doubt through those months of darkness he
was being brought to a deep consecration and, more
than that, an utter dependence upon God that was
to be the mark of all his following days.

It may also be that he was knowing something of
the experience of George Fox, who was "baptized
into the condition of all men," the sin of humanity
in all its depth revealed in one human heart, giving
a concern and a compassion for the needs of those
around him who knew not Christ.

On various occasions Chambers issued a warning
against the imitation of the experience of some
great soul. What Paul, Augustine, Luther, and oth-

ers went through were classic examples of how God could deal with souls in their desperate need, but they are not to be slavishly imitated. So we believe Chambers would not want any seeking soul to go through the long agony that was his until he came out into the glorious sunshine of the redeeming Christ. On the other hand, his experience is a challenge to all for whom conversion and even sanctification have been but glib and superficial expressions.

Perhaps the most helpful comment on this tremendous experience is found in some words written many years afterward, in a letter to a friend:

> God grant you may never need to be disciplined as He has disciplined me. He has taken me through Sheol and a broken heart. In those days of agony beyond words (if you knew, you would understand that pain must ever be the price of power), I wrote a few lines. I have never thought of them since, but they come back again to me now freshly; they are fragments torn from deep down—

Hush! There comes the sound of weeping,
Of my spirit vainly seeking,
Through the passions that are sweeping
Another sphere.
And its pained voice ever calling,
And its great tears ever falling,
Rack my life with fear.
Never can I live in gladness,
Never can I turn from sadness,
But must dwell in tears.

> After that I found my Lord, who sanctified me.

4

The Ministry

The Wandering Prophet (1906–1910)

From the day that deliverance came, after the great spiritual crisis at Dunoon, Oswald Chambers realized that God had a work, a special work, for him to do. The treasures of darkness revealed to him in those difficult days were now to be shared with others. Having served his spiritual apprenticeship, he was to launch out as a craftsman for God, a workman that need not be ashamed.

Years before he had written, "I feel I shall be buried for a time, hidden away in obscurity; then suddenly I shall flame out, do my work, and be gone."

The coming years were to see him as "An Apostle of the Haphazard," a title given to him by a missionary in Egypt. His attitude during this period is expressed in some words written as he ventured forth into God's service:

It came so clearly to me that in all ventures for God I had to go in faith, and now I do the same. It will be a great and joyful thing to see how God will open up the way. I never see my way; I know

God who guides, so I fear nothing. I never have farseeing plans, only confident trust.

During these four years Chambers was indeed a wandering prophet, not making his own plans nor following his own impulses, but moving under the compelling constraint of the hand of God. (His views on guidance were crystallized at this time in talks given in America and published in the booklet *Discipline of Divine Guidance*.)

On November 5, 1906, Oswald Chambers landed in New York, accompanied by a remarkable Japanese Christian, Bishop Juji Nakada, with whom he had formed a close fellowship. They had met at a convention in Scotland and were drawn to each other in the things of the Spirit. They also shared a delicious sense of humor. Nakada relates how one day "looking up at him I said, 'You are long like a poker.' With a laugh he looked down at me and said, 'Well, you are short, like a shovel, and it takes both ends to make a fire.' "

The six months in the States were for Chambers times of memorable fellowship with God's people. He was greatly used to bring many into a deep experience of the grace of God and the power of the Spirit.

That this brilliant and deeply spiritual man of God was not beyond a simple delivery, but effective in evangelism is proved by an incident that he recalled in a letter to his sister:

We had a very touching incident in the mission last Sunday. A dreary, dirty, desolate, drunken Scotsman came in, about thirty-four years of age. He was deeply convicted of sin. He staggered to the altar and in strong Scotch tones poured out his woes. As I knelt down by him, he turned his bloodshot eyes and tortured face to me with a look of unutterable pathos. I had spoken to him in broad Scotch—"What ails ye at the Lord, mon? Let Him hae His way wi' ye or ye'll hae to dree yer weird." The mother tongue touched him; he grasped my hand. "I'm frae Glasgie—dae ye think He'll save me?" "I'm frae Aberdeen way, and He's saved me," I said, and down we went on our knees, and after he beat the altar in an agony of conviction, God saved his soul. I have seen him since—unrecognizable, a handsome-looking young fellow, splendidly built and well educated.

During these days, his letters and diaries reveal an increasing sense of the presence of God under all circumstances. He writes to his sister:

> I wish I could convey to you the overpowering sense of God's love and protection as "my Father." I have met nothing strange; all treat me as friend and brother—Negro, Jap, Red Indian, American. I feel unspeakably at home among men, now that I know God. Glory to His name!

The next stage was a visit to Japan and a gracious time among the mission stations there. The diaries of the voyage to Japan make fascinating reading. Chambers gave himself to reading, and we note among the authors on his list at this time were George MacDonald (for whom he had a great love), Walter Scott, and Crockett; also, more serious, Westcott's *Gospel of the Resurrection* and David Smith's *Days of His Flesh*. There were seven Yale students on board, and Chambers found much delight in talking to them, and still more in praying for them. On the boat he celebrated his thirty-third birthday and was touched by the attentions of his worldly-minded fellow travelers.

In Japan, strenuous ministry was resumed, and Chambers found uplifting fellowship with the devoted missionaries of the Oriental Missionary Society and the Japan Evangelistic Band, especially Mr. and Mrs. Charles Cowman, two valiant warriors in the cause of Christ. Then came the voyage home, the most memorable part of which was passing Mount Sinai up the Suez Canal:

It is night now; a great pall has settled on all that wild, majestic desolation, and the wall of cliffs and desert mountains facing the afterglow from the African side looks like the pillar of fire. Nothing but the tongue of an inspired writer could avail to convey the day's impressions on me. I encamped with the children of Israel "before Pihahiroth, between Migdol and the Sea," and crossed the Red Sea with them in the breathless awe inspired by that miraculous east wind that clove the deep into a highway for the people of God. I danced a veritable Highland fling as Moses sang his imperial glory song, and shouted as Miriam and her women added their tribute. For three long weary days I wandered with them to Marah and heard their wild and fierce murmurings. I ate manna and reveled myself at Elim's palms. I trudged with eerie caution in the wilderness of sin and skirted round Sinai. I spent the forty days and nights on that uncouth awesome height with Moses. . . .

Little did he know as he sailed past the coast of Egypt that a few years later that would be his final scene of service.

The remaining three years of this period of min-

istry were spent in Britain (with the exception of
another short trip to America), and were devoted to
continuous travel as God opened the way for service. At Dunoon, Chambers had come into close
contact with the League of Prayer, founded by
Reader Harris, Q.C., a most remarkable and
gifted layman, who was concerned to encourage
church members to band together and pray for revival, emphasizing especially the message of the
Holy Spirit. Through this movement, with which
he had so much in common, Oswald Chambers
found continual opportunity for ministry. The fact
that the League of Prayer encouraged its members to stay in their churches produced many
openings in the pulpits of various denominations.
Doctor Dinsdale Young, the veteran Methodist
stalwart who claimed to have "discovered" Chambers in his Dunoon days, often invited him to his
London pulpit.

Many homes were open to this prophet of the
Lord, and although his message was stern and un-
compromising, in the homes he was humble, gracious, and ready to enter into the family life, especially that of the children. The writer remembers
Chambers coming to preach and hold mission services in his father's church. How natural and yet
how real he was. No pious platitudes, but straight
and yet loving words. Once my mother said to him
before a meeting, "We hope you will have a good
time, Mr. Chambers," to which he promptly replied,
"Yes we will, if we behave ourselves, and allow the
Lord to help himself to us." Another memorable yet
trivial incident: upon being asked, "What hinders
you most in the Christian life?" he replied, "Those,"
pointing to his Bible and notebooks.

The Dedicated Teacher: The Bible Training College (1911–1915)

Oswald Chambers was both a prophet and an evangelist, but he also had the gift of the teacher. He loved to teach (and that is usually the mark of a good teacher). At Dunoon he had a period of profitable experience in biblical and other instruction. Now during the interim years there came the vision of a Bible College where he could impart some of the truths that had become vital to him.

It came about in this way: The leader of the League of Prayer had a concern for such a place of spiritual training, and obviously Oswald Chambers was the man to act as principal. In 1910, Chambers had married Gertrude Hobbs, a gracious and gifted woman. She proved an ideal partner for someone dedicated to the work of God in this special way. A fine building was acquired facing Clapham Common; it was ideal for the purpose, the large double drawing room providing an excellent lecture hall, and the whole building capable of housing about twenty-five people.

The college was opened on January 12, 1911. It must be remembered that in those days the idea of such a community center for Bible teaching was almost unknown. (The one exception possibly would have been the Bible Training Institute in Glasgow, founded after Moody's visit to Scotland, and run along American lines, catering to a large student body.)

The whole venture was based on faith and prayer. To begin with there was only one resident student. Along with the principal and lady superintendent (Mrs. Chambers), this student had meals at a little square table set like an oasis in the desert of the big dining room. Later she was to testify of the amazing blessing of those days that might have been so embarrassing. That first student was later to go forth to be a valiant warrior for Christ in the Congo.

Soon the college began to fill up. The average number of students was about twenty-five, fairly evenly divided between men and women. The students were a mixed company. One, writing years later from the heart of China, recalled those early days: "I looked around on my first day, seated at the long table in the dining room, and I thought we must be the quaintest collection of people that had ever gathered together in a training school—men and women of all ages and occupations and social classes. Somehow the principal managed to weld us all into a very united family."

There were no entrance exams, and no external examinations were taken. Those who came were drawn by a spiritual hunger and a desire to equip themselves for Christ's service. There was nothing of pious sentimentality, but a strong compulsion in the very atmosphere that made each student seek the highest at all costs.

The days were very full. Up before six o'clock, the principal would be in his study preparing for the day, and the whole climate of the college was filled with the presence of God as he continually prayed that it might be, "from the attic to the basement." One from Australia wrote years afterward:

Every memory of my days at the BTC is a fresh cause for praise and thanksgiving to God. Morning worship was in itself a ministry. Always on time, the bell rang for the early morning assembly for prayer. Not infrequently as the students assembled he would be playing softly on the organ in the lecture room some such glad morning hymn as

When morning gilds the skies,
My heart awaking cries:
May Jesus Christ be praised!

Prayer was always a mighty factor with him, and when he led us in prayer we felt how truly he expressed to God for us what we hardly knew ourselves but realized to be our very prayer as he gave it voice.

One comment in the syllabus issued is worthy of notice:

The college provides atmosphere and time for spiritual life to take root before it is placed in the full blaze of the intellectual problems and actual difficulties of the times in which we live. It also provides a place of spiritual recuperation for ministers, missionaries, etc., who are "pressed beyond measure" and need time to get readjusted before God spiritually.

The training was essentially biblical in nature. Subjects studied included Bible Content, Biblical Psychology and Ethics, and Practical Christian Work. A college, however, cannot be judged by its prospectus and promised curriculum. The twofold test is the quality of the lectures and the character of the students as they go forth. As to the first, the lecture notes so faithfully recorded and published later in his books proved the abiding worth of the material supplied to the groups of eager students more than eighty years ago. As to the second test, the witness of those who once sat at the feet of Oswald Chambers is that of lives transformed and enriched and ready to face any circumstance at home or on the mission field.

The motto of the college (reflecting Chambers' love of Scotland and the Covenanters) was FOR CHRIST'S CROWN AND COVENANT. Kathleen Ashe in her delightful booklet *The Book of the College*, writes in her beautiful style:

> This student, at least, says from the heart with all the honest sternness of a balanced scrutiny, that throughout the years of the college life, in their passing and in retrospect, the figure of the Son of God—crowned and glorified—with the thorns and the nailprints and the hastening feet, drawing hearts rapt in a personal passionate devotion to himself, into the glimpsing of an understanding of the heart of God (an understanding that is as it were the first fringe of what is meant by His covenant in Christ, with its inevitable human covenant of a personal holiness manifesting itself in a life of service)—*that* figure, that voice, that face, is what emerges and stands and abides when all the rest: wonderful, agonizing, mystical, sinful, human, pitiful; great and obvious, gay and lighthearted; strong, weak; of laughter and of tears; of beauty and of utter hideousness—falls away, leaving only the Lord himself in covenant with all that we call our life, which is of the things unseen. . . . Eternal.

The Man Among Men: Egypt (1915–1917)

In July 1915, the Bible Training College was closed "for the period of the war."

On October 12, 1915, Oswald Chambers sailed for Egypt with the Mediterranean Expeditionary Force to join the staff of the YMCA. He was located at Zeitoun, seven miles from Cairo, and was joined in December by Mrs. Chambers and their daughter, Kathleen, along with their devoted helper, Mary Riley. Several of the BTC students also were allowed military permits to join in the work among the troops. That the women and child were allowed through at such a time was quite unusual, but was indeed a providential supply, for the need was tremendous.

It is hard for us to realize today the conditions that prevailed during that war period in the Near East. The pitiless heat, the fierce, relentless sun, the scorching sand, the insects—flies and insatiable mosquitoes—were a continual trial to the men and also to those who had gone out to help them. For the troops, however, it was the terrible monotony that told upon their nerves and their minds. Again, communications were not what they are today—no letters, no parcels—often for weeks, sometimes for months. If illness occurred, a man was sent to the camp hospital, a hot journey to Cairo or Alexandria, followed perhaps by a convalescent camp—but never was anyone sent home. Some in addition had faced the hardships and frustrations of the Dardanelles. It was to men facing all these hardships that Oswald Chambers ministered. Many, it was said, were saved from insanity only by the beauty and eternal freshness of the desert dawns and sunsets.

Zeitoun was a vast base camp of the Australian and New Zealand Forces (the famous Anzacs). There were also English and Scottish troops and some yeomanry. The camp was set up on the open desert: tents and tents and tents, horse lines, wagons, ambulances, and again tents, all set against the Eastern skies and the vast open spaces of air and light.

The YMCA hut was a large one built of matting nailed to a wooden staging, with the sand of the desert for a floor. The Egypt General Mission had their headquarters at Zeitoun and proved a great help in many ways, not the least in the building of a bungalow inside their compound. This became the home of Oswald Chambers and his family and helpers, but it was much more than that, for as he himself once wrote:

> Every house of God is a gate of heaven where the impossible and the miraculous become the natural breath.

Oswald Chambers had to find his way into this new life. In the large hut he found notices on the walls with all kinds of prohibitions. These all came down, as well as the small card announcing that there would be a short prayer meeting in the secretary's office each night. That was not the way of Chambers. From the first night he was in charge. At 8:45 P.M. he stood on the platform and, in a voice that could be heard across the desert, announced that in fifteen minutes' time prayers would be conducted for those who cared to stay. Most of the men shuffled out, but one or two stayed. Within a few weeks there were more staying than leaving the hut, and the forthright approach of the new secretary was appreciated by most, if not by all.

Each night Oswald Chambers conducted a class

for Bible study. Night after night the tent set aside for this was filled with men eager to hear the message of this man of God who brought with him such a sense of Christ's presence, yet with no mawkish piety about it.

After the lectures there would be leisured talks among the men strolling about in the quiet of the desert starlight or on the bungalow verandah. Then came family prayers with a circle of kneeling figures, including those who had stayed for fellowship and counsel.

Sundays were halcyon days. There was a service at eleven o'clock in the devotional hut, usually with a message leading up to the Lord's Table. At teatime the canteen was open as usual, but no charge was made. Chambers felt that this was a way of honoring God's day and proving the way of faith. Supplies for the hundreds of meals came in gifts from the homeland. Then at 7:30 P.M. in the big hut, the evening service was held, always a memorable time. Several of the staff were gifted soloists and contributed their talents. "It was great to see the faces of the men in the press and suffering of life's fight, change and lose their worry lines as the voices rang out in song; great also to be among them as they came out at the close of the service and to know the atmosphere they would carry with them into the coming week in the camp."

On Sunday it was not unusual for Chambers to have four services. Early each morning, he walked across to Aotea, a large New Zealand convalescent home—quite a long walk under those conditions. Then in the evening he would sometimes preach in

Cairo, and later take a soldiers' service at Ezbekieh Gardens.

But it was the personal unconscious influence of Chambers that counted most. As one has said: "Two salient features stamped upon that life were the absolute stern standard of the simplicity of walking in the light 'with nothing folded' before God—that for each one as for all that call to be 'my utmost for His highest' must always vibrate there—and the untroubled heart of a life lived in the haphazard of each day as from the hand of God. . . . And ever the joy that was in his heart, to whom all looked for inspiration and guidance, was the very joy of the Lord, triumphant over pain, weariness, thwarting and delay, disappointments and hindrances."

The impression given, reading through the diaries written for friends at home, is of a life of continuous activity lived in the most testing conditions, but lived in such a way that all who saw it found inspiration and blessing.

This is beautifully expressed in *The Book of the Bungalow*, written by Kathleen Ashe, that gifted woman who served in Egypt during the war and afterward. This record was intended only for those who knew "the bungalow," which was such a center of joy and blessing. Here is Miss Ashe's tribute:

Those who know the desert lands understand in a special way the words "as the shadow of a great rock in a weary land," and I think in looking back that it was not so much the joyous confident life of the place itself, nor the home so generously shared, nor the presence and the inspiration of Kathleen and her mother, and of Mary and the others all about in simple unaffected ways, nor even the inspiration of the teaching and of the services, but rather *himself* that made a strength for men's hearts both there and as they turned their thoughts back to the compound from march and camp and trench and dugout. It is a mighty thing to see even once in a lifetime a man, the self-expression of whose being is the redemption of Jesus Christ manifested in daily, hourly living. He would have called himself "a believer in Jesus." Face the words with heart and brain in accordance with the New Testament revelation, and one understands something of how it was God made himself through His servant "a refuge from the storm" to many and many a one . . . and how it is that through his written words the Lord himself is still touching the spirits of men.

Again, speaking of the actual family life, which meant so much to men exiled from home:

The bungalow was a very gay and happy place during this year—full of jocund gaiety and freedom from strain of all sorts despite the extraordinary demands made upon both of them—demands to drain all strength from life not built upon and drawn from the life of God alone.

Think what this atmosphere must have meant to men coming jaded and weary—morose and heartsick from the monotony of their days up the line! The very fact of there being still in existence a happy homelife where the simple courtesies and lovelinesses that make up gentle interaction were natural, came like a spring of cool water in a dry and thirsty land to many a heart where hope was growing veiled and dim, and despair's gnawing pain familiar in her stead. To other men losing grip upon their loyalty to the folks at home, beginning to yield to the temptations that beset men circumstanced as they, its influence often brought a challenge with the very voice of God.

The strain of the two years spent under such conditions was not revealed until the final break came. Perhaps the best picture of the day-by-day life can be given by quoting the closing pages of the diary. We note the continuous output of spiritual teaching, and the steady intake of thought and ideas through the reading that filled up the odd moments, the continual counseling of seeking souls, and most of all the atmosphere of praise and prayer, with the unfailing recognition of the amazing beauty of the sky, morning and evening. But let Chambers speak for himself through the entries of his closing days:

October 15. A very hazy but beautiful morning. Chapter 4 of Amos has some extraordinary terms—blasting and mildew and disease and pestilence and error and wrong being ascribed to God is exceptional (vv. 9–10). Verse 13 is a great adjunct to a man's thinking, mainly, that the powers beyond the control of man and all the consequences are in the powerful hand of God, and are not of blind cause and effect.

The evening class was good and well attended; we had a visit from some Welsh boys from the hospital who quite spontaneously broke into hymn singing, and we closed in prayer before they went off. The night is grand.

October 16. A glorious morning, the east is like a celestial scheme of shot silk, very elaborate and grand. Amos's prophecy is surely the most beautiful in diction; some of his imagery is splendid indeed. "Seek him that maketh the seven stars and Orion, and turneth the shadow of death into the

morning, and maketh the day dark with night"
(5:8). And the solemnity of the reiterated warn-
ings in verses 18–20.

October 17–18. There was no opportunity to fin-
ish last night. Ezbekieh Gardens was good, and
so was the padre's meeting here. Today is one of
the very finest days we have had, beautiful air
and clear, unsullied sunshine.

The class this evening was good and well attended, and the new moon a wonderful delight.

October 19–21. These days have to be slumped
together through lack of opportunity for writing.
The weather has been ideal and the sun glorious.
Friday night's class was keenly attentive. The
studies in Ecclesiastes have stirred up great interest.

As there is every prospect of my going up the
line shortly, it is time some of these saints got broken into taking the classes, so Biddy took the
class Saturday night and the service this morning, which was peculiarly radiant with His presence.

The free tea was fairly full. Mr. Swan (E.G.M.)
spoke with vigor and enthusiasm at the service;
there was a fine crowd of men and they listened
well. We had quite a big gathering for our sup-
pertime, and Sergeant Clarke bade us goodbye as
he expects to be sent up the line immediately. He
and Corporal Roy have been two of our most faithful friends out here; each night for nearly two
years they have come over from Cairo to the class.

October 23. The dawn this morning was like a
chalice held in the hand of God, full of the elixir
of life that coruscated in the most wonderful col-
ors. The whole day went splendidly; Mr. Swan's
subject in the evening took well and we had more
men and much liberty. I have read two books the

last few days, very different but both well worth referring to. One is Marmaduke Pickthall's *Children of the Nile*. Pickthall is to my mind the best and most unpretentious analyzer of this people. The other is Rider Haggard's *The Brethren*. It is really a noble idealization of supreme emotions.

October 26. The day has been most boisterously windy, but the early morning was like a vestibule to the audience chamber of the Almighty. I have been living in wonderful realms these days in a steady involuntary recalling of the Psalms. I have also read with immense delight Barrie's *The Little Minister*; his caustic humor is surely a gift, the rarest of the rare.

October 27. The day has been unusual but beautiful. Mr. Swan took the prayer meeting. Personally I do not think it possible to exaggerate the value of the prayer meeting and the going over of the men's names on the list individually. The shield of God has been very real today.

Sunday, October 28. It is two years today since I began in this region in the old hut, Zeitoun II, with Atkinson and Mackenzie and Cumine. In the early morning the passing of an Eastern night before the dawn brought out all its characteristics— limitless silver, gray-black shadows, dim white walls, violet blue skies. There is no idea of distance, and it is a thing to be witnessed.

Within three weeks of these words being written, Oswald was taken suddenly ill, and rushed to Gizeh Red Cross Hospital in Cairo. An operation for appendicitis was followed by a partial recovery and then a relapse. On November 15, God took him.

Some of us, young as we were, remember the shock of the news, conveyed by the cable sent with such courage and faith—"Oswald in His Presence."

The memorial service held on November 18, 1917, was indeed one of praise in the midst of grief. Let one who was there describe it for us:

> The large hut of the YMCA center was transformed that Sunday evening, as it had been every Sunday for months past, from a mere canteen to a real place of worship, both in appearance and atmosphere. But on this Sunday evening, all remembered the one who had worked in that place for so long and had made it a very real home in every sense for so many men of our armed forces. We gathered together under a sense of our irreparable loss and looked for the face that always shone with so much light, but we found it not, for Oswald Chambers had passed on, and we were without him who had been guide, counselor, and friend.
>
> The service all through was one of glad triumph and thanksgiving for the life that had been taken, and, in memory of him, we reconsecrated our lives to the Master whom he loved above everything else and obeyed without question. Through the singing of the hymn *God Is Our Refuge and Our Strength*, the realization came afresh with overpowering conviction, even with our loss, that God was with us yet. Words of real testimony were given by different ones of how, when groping in the dark, Mr. Chambers had guided them to Jesus Christ. Their testimonies were only a sample of what might be given by hundreds of our fighting men. Sidrak Effendi spoke in a most touching and affectionate way of Mr. Chambers and his good teaching, and how gentle he had been with him and with the Egyptian servants.

On the simple stone in Old Cairo Cemetery are

the words "A believer in Jesus Christ," and below this, a Bible opened at Luke 11:13, the promise that had meant so much to him and to many through him.

THE MESSAGE

In these brief chapters an attempt is made to crystallize the vital elements in the teaching of Oswald Chambers.

Students of his works will realize how much is omitted. More detailed treatment would involve aspects of the common evangelical heritage, such as prayer (*To Them That Ask*) and faith (*Not Knowing Whither*) and the work of the Holy Spirit (*He Shall Glorify Me*). Indeed, there is no part of the Christian faith on which he does not make some concise comment.

5

The Mind Behind the Man

Oswald Chambers was a student and a scholar. Although his messages are essentially spiritual and devotional, there is behind them all a background of deep study and wide reading.

Taking an arts course at Edinburgh, he studied logic, psychology, and philosophy. These subjects he continued to study and teach during the years at Dunoon.

Of the influences on his thinking, none is greater than that of P. T. Forsyth, of whom he wrote in April 1907:

> I am forcibly struck with Dr. Forsyth's book on New Theology. He has some mighty things to say, and God is at the heart of them. His stream will become clearer as it runs if people don't haul him up too suddenly and make him explain himself. He will say something that will mark this epoch if his time is not wasted explaining what he means to people who won't think.

This probably refers to Forsyth's *Positive Preaching and the Modern Mind*, published in 1907. It is striking that years afterward, Chambers' talks on "The Shadow of an Agony" are headed with quota-

tions from Dr. Forsyth. He realized the place that
Forsyth was to occupy in later days when all the furor of the R. J. Campbell New Theology had passed.
Another influence was undoubtedly that of Dr.
James Denney, whose emphasis on the theology of
the Cross meant so much in the days of the First
World War.

In the realm of psychology, the influence of
William James is very evident, and Chambers
draws on his practical teaching on habit formation
and on mental concentration. The psychology of the
natural man, however, did not interest Oswald
Chambers so much as "the psychology of the new
man in Christ." The whole of his "biblical psychology" is the exposition of the psychology of the
Christ-centered personality. In the diaries written
in Egypt there are frequent references to the writings of J. H. Jowett, John Hutton, and T. R. Glover
(whose *Jesus of History* made a deep impression).
An account of a meeting with Dr. Rendal Harris,
who had landed in Egypt after being torpedoed, is
of great interest. Chambers found he had much in
common with this saintly modern scholar.

Oswald Chambers was a great Christian thinker.
He was concerned that much modern thinking in
his day was non-Christian. He believed that a fullorbed Christian life involved not only living as a
Christian but *thinking as a Christian*. He advocated wide reading as a basis for wise thinking.

Here we quote from Dr. Coggan:

When that wise leader of men, Oswald Chambers, was seeking to help a man who found himself in a mental cul-de-sac, Chambers asked him
what he read. The man replied that he read noth-

ing but the Bible and books directly associated with it. Chambers replied, "The trouble is you have allowed part of your brain to stagnate for want of use," and forthwith proceeded to give his friend a list of over fifty books—philosophical, psychological, theological—covering almost every phase of current thought. The result was a revolution that could only be described as a mental new birth. Chambers wrote later to his friend: "When people refer to a man as 'a man of one book,' meaning the Bible, he is generally found to be a man of multitudinous books who simply isolates the one book to its proper grandeur. The man who reads only the Bible does not as a rule know it—or human life."[1]

In actual fact, Chambers was indeed "a man of one book," and beyond all his specialized reading in theology, etc., there was a concentration on the Book. He ever gave it the first place and to study it was his greatest delight. He would say to his students, "Ransack your Bibles." All his works show an unusual grasp of Scripture. For the minutiae of detailed critical study, he had little time. The Word meant so much to him that he had no patience with those who treated it simply as "any other book" or even as great literature.

He wrote from Cincinnati on his American tour in 1907:

I find myself removed daily more and more from sympathy, even in possibility, with those who look at the Bible as mere literature. It is more than life to me consciously. Also I am growing more and more grateful for the tremendous—

---

[1]*Stewards of Grace*, p. 49 (H.& S.).

and as I once thought unnecessary—schooling I gave myself in philosophy and psychology in my Edinburgh and Dunoon days; I see now that the mental discipline was invaluable for God's work.

Perhaps we can best illustrate his attitude toward Scripture by a series of short quotations, some of them *obiter dicta* given during his lectures and talks.

"The Word" is Jesus himself (John 1:1); therefore we must have an experiential knowledge of Him before we understand the literal words of the Bible.

Our attitude toward the Bible is a stupid one; we come to the Bible for proof of God's existence, but the Bible has no meaning for us until we know God does exist. The Bible states and affirms facts for the benefit of those who believe in God; those who don't believe in God can tear it to bits if they choose.

People can dispute the words of the Bible as they like, but get a soul in whom the craving for God has come and the words of the Bible create the new life in him. "Being born again . . . by the word of God" (1 Peter 1:23).

The main characteristics that are the proof of the indwelling Spirit are an amazing tenderness in personal dealing and a blazing truthfulness with regard to God's Word.

The reason some of us are not healthy spiritually is because we don't use the Bible as the Word of God but only as a textbook.

The Bible does not thrill; the Bible nourishes. Give time to the reading of the Bible and the re-creating effect is as real physically as that of fresh air.

The statements of Scripture apart from the Holy Spirit's illumination are dull; it needs no spiritual insight to regard Jesus Christ as a man who lived beyond His time, but when I am born again I have insight into the person of Jesus, an insight that comes through communion with God by means of the Bible.

Beware of reasoning about God's Word; obey it.

We may sum up the thought and teaching of Chambers by saying it was essentially Christ-centered and Bible-based. He illustrates well the distinction he used to make between the *fanatic* and the *genius*; the former sees only one aspect of truth and clings blindly to it; the latter sees all but holds to that which is central. No wonder one who used to listen to him in Egypt said, "It seems when he speaks that a great light is shining." In that light many see new aspects of the truth as it is in Jesus.

6

The Poet and the Artist

Oswald Chambers was not only a student and a thinker, he was a poet and an artist. During his early struggles he often expressed his thoughts in simple poetic form. Here is one example:

"Prayer Pleading"

Oh take my heart, my Savior,
Move its inward springs for me,
Thy life in my behavior
Springs in actions constantly.
Oh, my Savior, I am mourning
For a living touch from Thee,
Let Thy Spirit's pure adorning
Mold my character in me.
Oh do hear me, Oh do hear me,
Else I think my heart will break.
In the longing, be Thou near me
And my burning thirst—oh slake.
Oh, Lord Jesus, hear my crying
For a consecrated life,
For I bite the dust in trying
For release from this dark strife.

He was a great lover of the poets in his early years, and it is interesting to note which writers seemed to mean the most to him. First and foremost was F. W. H. Myers, whose poem "St. Paul," and also the lesser known "John the Baptist" were often quoted. Then came the Brownings, Robert and Elizabeth, both of whom are quoted from time to time. A lesser known poetess, Mrs. Hamilton King, was another favorite, particularly "The Sermon in the Hospital," part of that remarkable study of the days of Mazzini in Italy ("The Disciples"), containing the words so applicable to Chambers himself:

> For himself,
> So shadowed forth in every look and act
> Our Lord, without whose name he
>   seldom spoke,
> One could not live beside him and forget.

Chambers' great love for literature is revealed in a letter to his sister when he was in the midst of a busy program in the USA, visiting Holiness camp meetings and the like.

> My box has at last arrived. My books! I cannot tell you what they are to me—silent, wealthy, loyal lovers. To look at them, to handle them, and to reread them! I do thank God for my books with every fiber of my being. Friends that are ever true and ever your own. Why, I could have almost cried for excess of joy when I got hold of them again. I see them all just at my elbow now—Plato, Wordsworth, Myers, Bradley, Halyburton, St. Augustine, Browning, Tennyson, Amid, etc. I know them; I wish you could see how they look at me, a quiet calm look of certain acquaintance.

Chambers' use of the poets in quotations is more marked in his earliest booklets. For example, *The*

Discipline of Loneliness, brought out before the
war. In this brief study of only sixty-six pages, there
are some thirty quotations from the poets woven
most effectively into the message. Of these, no less
than seven are from F. W. H. Myers, five from
Browning, two from George MacDonald, two from
Mrs. Hamilton King ("The Disciples"), two from
F. R. Havergal, two from Shelley, and one from each
of the following: Milton, Tennyson, Matthew
Arnold, Faber, Harriet Beecher Stowe, T. T. Lynch,
A. Proctor, and Elizabeth Barrett Browning.

The style of his later writings, lectures to students and to servicemen, precluded the more literary setting but it is still present. Of his last series
of talks, those on Job took their title from Browning
(*Baffled to Fight Better*), and those on Ecclesiastes
from Francis Thompson (*Shade of His Hand*).

That his love of the poets and their message remained with him is evident in a special lecture he
gave to the men in Egypt a few months before his
death. The outline is worth a look, for it shows his
gift of linking biblical truth with secular literature.

I. The Poem of Imagination: Psalm 45:1; 2 Peter
   1:21
   The interpretation of actual existence ex-
   pressed in the medium of human emotions.
   A. "The Beyond That Is Within"
      Illus. "Domine Illuminatio Mea"
      "Daffodils" (Wordsworth)
   B. "The Beauty That Lies in Words"
      Illus. "Ode to a Grecian Urn" (Keats)
      "Lady of Shallott" (Tennyson)
      N.B. Why there is value intrinsic in move-
      ment, dancing, rhythm, singing, and ges-

       tures; periodicity in nature, tides, seasons, etc.

C. "The Blessing of Wonder"
   Illus. "Perfect Woman" (Wordsworth)
   "Ancient Mariner"

D. "The Bane of Woe"
   Illus. "A Fond Kiss" (Burns)
   "Fountain of Tears" (Arthur O'Shaughnessy)
   N.B. Poetry must please through the sense of beauty.

II. The Poem of Identification: John 7:20–24
The interpretation of actual humanity expressed in divine union: 2 Corinthians 3:2; 1 John 3:3.

III. The Poem of Incarnation: Proverbs 8:22–36
The interpretation of actual deity expressed in human flesh: John 1:1–14.

It has been said that for the saint there is a conversion from nature to grace, and then there must be a reconversion from grace to nature. Oswald Chambers knew something of this. In his later days, while remaining intensely spiritual and passionately devoted to his Lord, there seems to have been a revival of interest in art and literature, which for a time had been completely laid aside. He expresses this himself in some words written on his forty-third birthday (July 24, 1917).

There comes to me growingly a sense of the "externals" of things. Perhaps the plunging horror and conviction of sin in my early life not only disrupted my art calling and all the tendencies of those years but switched me off by a consequent swing of the pendulum away from external beauties of expression in form and color and rhetoric, and made me react to the rugged and uncouth and unrefined. But now I seem to have the experience Ruskin refers to: his grief at realizing the loss of his appreciation of the beauty of an English hedgerow, and his sad wonder if he would ever have the old emotions back again; then his recurrent joy and bounding delight when he found it all came back with redoubled force in later life. That perhaps states it. The beauty of form, of expression, of color, all the fleeting "features of the immense external fields of life," are again delighting me marvelously. The old delight is back in a glorious *edition de luxe*, as it were. It is no longer an individual delight but a personal one, without the lust to possess, and without the forced detachment of the spectacular, yet with all the complete delight that possesses a child's mind in things. My inner career at the beginning was heavy and strong, even lurid and agonizing in the earlier phases; latterly, austere and peaceful, and now it is merging into a joy that is truly the receiving of an hundredfold more.

Had he lived on, Oswald Chambers might well have realized his youthful ambition to do something for the redemption of the aesthetic kingdom—music, art, and poetry; to bring to these realms the message of a redeeming Christ, even as C. S. Lewis, in our day, has done a similar work in the realm of literature. Writing to a friend in his very early days, Chambers said: "Be fervent in your fighting against those who would put art in place of religion; art can never take satisfactorily the place of religion, but may be pursued in the religious spirit."

7

The Fundamentals of His Faith

During his days in Egypt, Oswald Chambers gave some remarkable talks later published under the title *The Shadow of an Agony*. We feel that in some ways these lectures, delivered in the midst of war conditions, give Chambers' fundamental philosophy.

There is no explicit personal note (Chambers rarely spoke in public of himself or of his own spiritual experience, nor, for that matter, in private), but we imagine that here in some measure are presented the steps by which he found his way through to a living and vital faith. No doubt close contact with men facing death amid the horrors of war emphasized the questions that often lurk in the back of men's minds and that only come to the surface under the pressure of urgent circumstances.

The first insistence is on a right attitude of mind and heart before we approach the holy ground. The true approach is often through personal suffering, at least through an awareness of life's tragedy. Ultimately, life is not rational and cannot be explained by mere logic. The keynote is

REDEMPTION, which is God's way of dealing with
man's tragic plight.

> No man can redeem the world; God has done it;
> redemption is complete. That is a revelation, not
> something we conclude by thinking; and unless
> we grant that redemption is the basis of human
> life, we will come up against problems for which
> we can find no way out. The thing that will need
> to be restated after the war, theologically, is re-
> demption; at present "redemption" is not in the
> vocabulary of the average earnest man.

Jesus Christ is God manifest in the flesh. He
alone can redeem the human race—and He has
done it.

Forgiveness means that God turns an unholy one
into a holy one by putting within him a new disposition altogether. Chambers had no room for an
antinomian approach that gloried in an imputed
righteousness that was not also imparted. This is
summed up in trenchant words:

> The point about Christian forgiveness is not
> that God puts snow over a dunghill, but that he
> turns a man into the standard of the Forgiver.
> The great thing up to God is that in forgiving me
> He has to give me the heredity of His Son.

The reality of God's redeeming work does not
come home until we meet some tragic circumstance
and reach the limits of our moral life. When man's
life is going along smoothly and there is no sense of
sin or failure, the Cross of Jesus seems "much ado
about nothing." In the case of intense moral and
spiritual suffering, there comes a realization of the
need that God must do for man what he cannot do

for himself. There must however be a "coming to the end of ourselves." Jesus Christ and self-realization cannot exist together. Being a Christian does not mean understanding a plan of salvation (the *devil* understands that). A Christian is one who has received a new life through the Cross. "When I accept Jesus Christ's way, He transfigures me from within."

God for the Christian is not a series of abstract theological terms but One whose essential nature is holiness. The doctrine of the Incarnation means that God became the weakest thing in His own creation, a baby. What we know about God we accept as a revelation given to us through Jesus Christ by the Holy Spirit.

In this sense Chambers often stated that he was "an avowed agnostic"; all he knew about God had come not through reasoning but through accepting Jesus Christ and putting His words to the test.

The fundamental thing about Christianity is a personal relationship with Jesus Christ. The religion of Jesus Christ means that a man is delivered from sin into something that makes him forget all about himself. (The trick of pseudo-evangelism is that it drives a man into concentrated interest in himself.)

Christ came to make us what He teaches we should be.

For Oswald Chambers, the fundamentals[1] were

---

[1]In speaking of the fundamentals, we are not using the term in the "fundamentalist" sense of orthodox beliefs, but rather of those truths that were fundamental to Chambers' faith, and central among these is redemption. What was said of Henry Drummond (who also died in his early forties) might well be applied to Oswald Chambers: "There were some aspects of truth from which he stood reverently aside."

not certain orthodox beliefs to be rigidly held with a closed mind, but rather certain truths that had come alive through a divine/human encounter. To put it more simply, the Holy Spirit makes living and reality the basic truth of the Gospel; and they are *fundamental* in that they become the foundation of Christian thinking and living.

What then was Chambers' attitude toward the Atonement? A great student of his works has summed it up like this:

> Chambers did not deal with the Atonement in an objective way. He knew well the writings of the basic theologians, such as Forsyth, Denney, etc. He accepted the foundation truth of Scripture. "There is no other foundation laid than that is laid, Jesus Christ and Him crucified."

Our Lord's Cross is the gateway into His life. He refers to it many times, often simply in an emphatic sentence. But he gives his greatest thought to the outflow of that once-offered sacrifice—the redemption of the world. By His atoning death Jesus Christ put the whole human race on the basis of redemption. By accepting in childlike faith the fact that Jesus had made an all-sufficient Atonement for all, every man could step into a right initial relationship to God—ransomed, healed, restored, forgiven. On the sure ground of God's free grace the believing man is called upon to let Christ's redemption work out within his personality to the full recovery of his bit of human nature for God. (D.L.)

This emphasis on redemption, which is the basis of all Chambers' teaching, is illustrated by the following quotations (all taken from *My Utmost for His Highest*):

As workers for God, we have to get used to the revelation that redemption is the only reality.

Jesus Christ switched back the whole human race into right relationship to God. He put the basis of human life on redemption, i.e., He made the way for every son of man to get into communion with God.

Rehabilitation means putting the whole human race back into the relationship God designed for it, and that is what Jesus Christ does in redemption.

The creating power of redemption comes through the preaching of the Gospel, but never because of the personality of the preacher.

In the Cross of Christ, Jesus Christ redeemed the whole human race from the possibility of damnation through the heredity of sin.

Redemption means that Jesus Christ can put into any man the heredity disposition that was in himself.

Jesus Christ deliberately took upon His own shoulders and bore in His own person the amassed sin of the whole human race . . . and by so doing He put the whole human race on the basis of redemption.

Prayer is the working of the miracle of redemption in me that produces the miracle of redemption in others by the power of God.

8

The Pattern of Christian Experience

Perhaps the central feature in the teaching of Oswald Chambers is the insistence that the true pattern for the experience of the Christian is the life of Christ. The Christian ideal is not the outward and literal imitation of Jesus, *but the living out of the Christ-life implanted within by the Holy Spirit.*

Actually this principle is not unique in the literature of sanctity. Andrew Jukes (1815–1901), a writer of independent mind whose message in some ways anticipates Oswald Chambers (although we cannot trace any actual quotation from him), wrote: "As Adam is the type of our natural life, so is Christ the type or figure of the eternal life, which is by grace renewed in us. . . ."

Pascal (1623–1662), two hundred years before Jukes, has said that everything that happened in the life of Jesus Christ should take place in the experience of the true believer.

Henry Scougal (1650–1681), a devout young professor of King's College, Aberdeen, wrote a book published in 1692 under the title, *The Life of God in the Soul of Man.* It was to have a great influence on George Whitfield and the Wesleys in their Oxford days. Its title and its contents strike the note that we find at the heart of Chambers' teaching. Scougal gives a prayer for "one who had formerly entertained some false notions of religion and begins to discover what it really is." (Was this Scougal himself?) These are the closing words of the prayer:

> Blessed be thine infinite mercy, who sent thine own Son to dwell among men and instruct them by His example as well as by His laws, giving them a perfect pattern for what they ought to be. O that the holy life of the blessed Jesus may be always in my thoughts and before my eyes, till I receive a deep sense and impression of those excellent graces that shone so eminently in Him; and let me never cease my endeavors till that new and divine nature prevail in my soul and Christ be before me and within me.

We find another forerunner of this emphasis on the life of the indwelling Christ as the key to the believer's sanctification in the Puritan Walter Marshall (1628–1680), whose remarkable work *The Gospel Mystery of Sanctification* was rediscovered for the general reader by Andrew Murray, who at the end of the last century brought out an abridged edition (the complete work was reissued in modern form in 1854 by Oliphants).

It is significant that Oswald Chambers used Marshall's title as a subtitle for his booklet *Our Brilliant Heritage*, in which, without actual quotation, the essence of Marshall's teaching is conveyed, namely that sanctification is the very holiness of Jesus—His peace, His Joy, His purity, imparted to us by the Holy Spirit and received by faith.

But the thought goes back to the apostle Paul, who spoke of the indwelling Christ. "Christ in you, the hope of glory" (Colossians 1:27); "Christ, who is our life" (Colossians 3:4); "Christ liveth in me" (Galatians 2:20).

This essentially New Testament message is laid hold of and emphasized in the teaching of Chambers. In *The Psychology of Redemption*, and again, perhaps more deeply, in *Bringing Sons Unto Glory*, the parallel between our Lord's life and that of the Christian disciple is worked out in considerable detail.

Thus His unique birth was a coming, an advent, God entering human nature: "He did not come from the human race; He came into it from above." So our new birth means the coming of the divine life into our human personalities. Have we allowed our personal lives to become a "Bethlehem" for the Son of God?

> Though Christ a thousand times in
>   Bethlehem be born,
> But not within thyself, thy soul
>   will be forlorn.
>
> —Silesius

The years of silent growth, the "hidden years" in the life of our Lord (cf. Luke 2:40), represent the element of growth in the Christian life, not dependent on the passing of time but on surrender and obedience.

These should lead on to a crisis of complete consecration, symbolized by our Lord's baptism, an event which, as Chambers is careful to note, is unique in that He identified himself with sinful humanity that He might "take away the sin of the world." The response of the Father was a divine anointing, equipping Him for the great task of world redemption. We too, through the crisis of a complete surrender, may receive a divine anointing (cf. 1 John 2:20), preparing us for effective service. We, however, unlike our sinless Lord, need not only the holy anointing but also the cleansing fire (cf. Acts 2:3). Oswald Chambers always insisted on the need for "a mighty baptism of the Holy Spirit" as the birthright of every believer. In passing, we note that he never argued about this, but simply spoke out of his own tremendous experience, which he found verified in the Word of God. For him it was a vital part of the pattern.

The temptation of our Lord is a clue to the type of testing to be expected, not by the natural man but by the regenerated. Even as the Son of God was tried on the line of doing His Father's will in his own way, i.e., by the appeal to the material, to the spectacular, and to the way of compromise with the world, so the sons of God, born of His Spirit, will find their loyalty and obedience tested.

The Transfiguration is the central event in the earthly life of Jesus Christ, when His glory shone forth and his intimate disciples became witnesses of His divine majesty. For the modern disciple, this suggests that place when we become aware of our Lord as He really is: "Almighty God presented in the guise of a human life." This vision is not enough in itself; it must be taken down into the valley and worked out there in the midst of devil-possessed humanity. This principle of obedience to the vision in spiritual life is continually stressed by Oswald Chambers. The "vision" of salvation and of sancti-fication may be sincerely grasped both intellectually and spiritually, and then fade because it is not expressed in action.

The Savior came down from the Mount and took the Calvary road: and so must we, if the pattern is to be worked out in our lives.

In the experience of the believer, the Cross stands for more than the place of forgiveness (which miracle of God's grace Oswald Chambers never minimizes; it is indeed, the foundation of all that follows). There must be a witness to be identified with Christ on the cross so that the words of Galatians 2:20: "I am crucified with Christ," are experientially true.

The Cross is then not only the secret of salvation but the place where we deny ourselves and (to use a favorite phrase of Oswald Chambers) "give up our right to ourselves."

Then follows the Resurrection. Out of death comes life, out of the life laid down comes fullness of life: thus for the disciple who has been not only *to* the Cross but *through* the Cross, there is life, abundant life. This is imparted to us in the gift of the Holy Spirit.

Finally, the Ascension completes what began on the Mount of Transfiguration. Our Lord, having "emptied himself, and become obedient unto death, even the death of the cross," is now exalted to the throne and sends forth the Spirit upon His waiting followers. Thus we too may know what it is to ascend with Christ and to dwell in the heavenly places while we walk amid the dust of our daily pathway.

9

The Outworking in Christian Character

The emphasis on the expression of salvation in human life runs right through the works of Chambers. Take, for example, his *Studies in the Sermon on the Mount*, one of his earliest books to be published. Here we find no dilution of the dynamic demands of our Lord's teaching. Nor is there any suggestion that the Sermon on the Mount contains teaching for another dispensation. Chambers would rather have said that it was for "the dispensation of the Holy Ghost." This is the life that should be lived now by the man of God filled with the Spirit. In it are laid down principles that can only be put into action by those who have been born from above, but *they* must realize that here we have God's standard for daily living. We quote:

> Our Lord's message here is that the righteousness of the scribes and Pharisees was right, not wrong, and that His disciples were to exceed that righteousness. That the Pharisees did much more, and other than righteousness, is obviously clear, but our Lord is here talking of their righteousness. What is it that exceeds right doing if it

be not right being? Right being, without doing
anything, is possible, but it cannot exceed the
righteousness of the scribes and Pharisees. The
way I can stop right doing is by refusing to enter
into relationship with God, both by His words and
His providences.

Chambers himself lived out the message. To take
one example, he insisted on fulfilling the command
"Give to him that asks." I remember at Perth Convention seeing him talking to a man, obviously a
scrounger, and coming away after handing him
something. "Yes," he said, "I gave him a shilling and
told him he did not deserve it, but I gave it because
my Master commanded me to, and if he went and
damned himself with it, it was not my concern." He
said that beggars were sent to us to try our faith.

Someone has outlined the life of Chambers in
terms of the Beatitudes:

He was poor in spirit—and actually poor.
He was a mourner—for multitudes on his
    prayer list; he knew he would be comforted
    about them.
He was meek—toward God, always accepting
    His dispensations for himself.
He hungered and thirsted after righteousness
    and was continually being filled.
He was merciful—with an abounding generosity.
He was pure in heart—and saw God at work.
He was a peacemaker—seeing an inner core of
    likeness in many varied groups.
He was persecuted for righteousness' sake—in
    the modern form of being set aside.
He was at times reviled and falsely criticized.
He was a city set on a hill, not to be hid, and a
    light for his generation.

He did trust the heavenly Father, like the birds,
and grew as the lily where he was put.
He asked and received as few have done in our
time.
He built on the Rock and no storm could shake
him.

The Natural Into the Spiritual

The expression of the Christ-life in human nature involved, according to Chambers, a turning of the natural into the spiritual by a series of moral choices. This has not always been understood by those seeking for the best and the highest in their spiritual lives. Deliverance from sin is not deliverance from human nature. There are things in our human nature that must be destroyed by neglect; there are other things that must be destroyed by active attack, that is by the divine strength imparted by God's Spirit.

God delivers us from sin; we have to deliver ourselves from individuality; that is, to present our natural life to God and sacrifice it until it is transformed into a spiritual life by obedience.

The natural life is not sinful, but there must be an attitude of surrender, of giving up "my right to myself," my natural independence and self-assertiveness. This is where the battle has to be fought. Things that are right and good from the natural standpoint may keep us back from God's best. Jesus said, "If any man will be my disciple, let him deny himself," i.e., his right to himself.

This very characteristic line of teaching found an answer in many hearts stirring to find the secret of sanctification in terms of daily living. One such at the close of a life of faithful service testified (in a letter to Mrs. Chambers) what it meant to him:

> When I first heard Chambers speak on *The Supreme Climb* in the life of Abraham, it described a critical stage in sainthood. Only slowly has the process of the natural into the spiritual in its true nature become evident. It is not the joyous intake of the Holy Spirit in His creative energy, nor that later climax when the "old man" is put off and the "new man" is put on (a great event in the soul's life), and all based on personal identification with Jesus Christ in His death and in His resurrection. Being transformed into the spiritual is *a process* not a climax, though striking occurrences will show how the matter is proceeding. Chambers described it in the strong terms: "Battered into shape and use by shocks of doom."

> They are a description of Paul's experience in 2 Corinthians 4, and the result is that the LIFE of Jesus is made manifest in his *mortal* flesh. The life of Jesus made manifest in our mortal flesh alone enables us to walk even as He walked (1 John 2:6).

This is one of the outstanding spiritual demands Chambers' teaching makes on us. When the Spirit of God gives us intuitive discernment, we see things in our own life and in others, not morally bad, but which we are called to pass by. And that intuitive light becomes the discipline of our lives. And so the good, natural things are transformed into the spiritual. The process began in me fifty years ago when I heard the Word applied: "While ye have the light, believe in the light, that ye may be the children of light" (John 12:36). It has been operating ever since through the mercy of God (D.L.).

10

The Outgoing in Christian Service

The Christian life must not only be worked out in daily living and habit. There must also be an outgoing in obedience and service. To every true disciple the Master says, "So send I you."

The book of the same title gives the main teaching of Chambers on this aspect of Christian discipleship. In a sense every believer is called to be a missionary. The scene of action is secondary. The main concern is obedience to His command.

The call of God is something definite and profound. This is shown in the following striking paragraph:

> The call of God is the call according to the nature of God; where we go in obedience to that call depends entirely on the providential circumstances that God engineers. The call of God is not a call to any particular service, although our interpretation of the call may be; i.e., my contact with the nature of God has made me realize what I can do for God. The call to service is the echo of my identification with God. My service is the outcome of what is fitted to my nature; God's call is

91

fitted to His nature, therefore I can never hear His call until I have received His nature.

As the call comes, the feeling "I am called to be a missionary" is a universal one; the Holy Spirit sheds abroad the love of God in my heart: "God so loved the world. . . ."

Once the call is realized there is a willingness for divine preparation. Through circumstances, often very humdrum conditions, and sometimes disagreeable people, God seeks to prepare His servants that they may be for Him "broken bread and poured out wine" (a favorite phrase of Chambers).

The realization of all that God has done brings with it a sense of obligation. Like Paul, we are debtors (Romans 1:14).

> When the realization comes home that Jesus Christ has served me to the end of all my meanness, my selfishness, and sin, then nothing I meet with from others can exhaust my determination to serve men for His sake. I am not to come among men as a superior person, I am to come among men as the love slave of Jesus Christ, realizing that if I am worth anything at all it is through His redemption.

As we respond to the call of God, He gives us a vision of what He would have us be and do for Him, but there is often a valley to go through before the vision is brought down to earth. Like Moses, we may need to go through a period of wilderness discipline before we can lead God's people forth. Both self-confidence and self-despising must be dealt with.

"The one great need for the missionary is to be

ready for Jesus Christ, and we cannot be ready unless we have seen Him."

This readiness implies a willingness for all of God's will, so that He can put us where He likes—in pleasant places or mean duties; but we are there for Him. There is no such thing as prominent service or obscure service, it is all one with God.

Missionary enterprise according to New Testament standards must be based "not on the pathos of pity but on the passion of obedience." More than the need of the people is the thought of the command of Christ. We go because He has given the command. The true missionary, at home or abroad, is one sent of Christ, God's Son, even as He was sent of the Father. The one thing that matters is to maintain a personal relationship with Jesus Christ. The work is His, and we are called to be true to *Him* and to carry out *His* enterprises.

The work of the missionary, according to Christ himself, is to "disciple all nations." It is not enough that men be saved; there must be a work of "discipling," and through lack of that the church at home and abroad has suffered much. "The first aim of missionary enterprise is the spiritual evangelization of the people, and the missionary must be united to Jesus by the spiritual bond of sanctification before he can really evangelize others."

Behind all true Christian service must, of course, be prayer. Chambers sums it up succinctly: *Prayer, the work* (John 14:12–14); *Prayer, the fruit* (John 15:16); and *Prayer, the battle* (Ephesians 6:11–20). The final secret of the Christian's outgoing in service is a sense of the mastery of the Master. It is out of love and loyalty to his Lord that the disciple goes out in service, and whatever treatment he receives goes on to the end. "We have to be entirely His and to exhibit His spirit no matter what circumstances we are in."

In words that Oswald Chambers loved and often quoted:

Christ! I am Christ's! and let the name suffice
     you.
Ay, for me too He greatly hath sufficed.
Lo, with no winning words I would entice you;
Paul has no honor and no friend but Christ.
Yea, thro' life, death, thro' sorrow and thro'
     sinning
He shall suffice me, for He hath sufficed:
Christ is the end, for Christ was the beginning;
Christ the beginning, for the end is Christ.

Epilogue:
The Continuance of the Message

Mrs. Oswald Chambers was called home on January 15, 1966. For almost fifty years she had given herself to the task of spreading the message left by her husband. It is possible now to speak more freely and intimately of the wonderful service she rendered through the years, making possible the reproduction and spreading abroad of Chambers' teaching.

We quote from letters written toward the close of November 1917.

God has so wonderfully been near and sustained. His Word has been so precious, making the unseen things so real and the only things that really matter. The words in my heart from him are on the memorial card—"Therefore are they before the throne of God and serve Him day and night in His temple." I do know that he is still serving in ways I cannot comprehend. The *Daily Light* spoke of a costly stone having been built into the temple, and I know he is where God would have him be, "a pillar" in the temple of my God to go out no more forever. . . . It's wonderful to be here in Luxor, and I am sure God's guidance will come all the time. . . . Kathleen is an unspeakable comfort and a sacred trust from God.

And again, writing from Wasta on the Nile:

I recall that Oswald used to say, "Thank God, He does give us something difficult to do," and I know that He will be sufficient and make His way plain before us. Just now His way will be to go on in Zeitoun, and there will be ample means of serving Him there. There is a very beautiful garden here and God has made it into a parable to me, especially that the trees which are now tall and grand have grown from seeds; and I feel as if that is how it will be with Oswald's life, that in many lives there will grow up the tree of the knowledge of God from the seeds of his teaching. I just feel as if I want to sow his books [widely] and it will be such a joy and privilege to send them around. . . . These days it is like beginning to walk by faith, like a little child, with many tumbles, but always the One near to help, and ever growing stronger and stepping out with more confidence.

The impetus to start spreading the message came when one of the workers showed Mrs. Chambers a copy of a Chambers message entitled "The Place of Help" (Psalm 121), and suggested that it might be printed and sent out to the men for Christmas. Countless letters had come in from men in the camps and up at the front expressing their grief at the loss of such a friend and teacher. So this leaflet was printed and sent out, many writing to speak of the comfort and blessing it had brought. Then the idea came of printing a talk and sending it out each month. With the help of the YMCA, this continued until May 1919, copies being sent out to every camp in Egypt and Palestine and France. This was how it all began.

Then the books began to appear. The main purpose was to cater to the men in the armed forces, along with other friends who had known Chambers. The first book issued was *Baffled to Fight Better*, that amazing study in Job, and then *The Shadow of an Agony* and others followed. There was no charge made for the books, but many gave gifts as a token of the blessing they received. This all brought a great sense of God's undertaking and of His purpose in the work and was an incentive to go forward with the publishing, and as one man put it, "to print and print until there's nothing more to print."

When the war was over and Mrs. Chambers, along with little Kathleen, returned to London, she was conscious that she had found her life work. In a private letter she wrote: "I am retyping *The Shadow of an Agony*. I find how much benefit I have still got from my old legal days; I mean getting into the habit of perfecting a thing by typing and retyping, and I am so glad to have had all that experience. . . . Living with Oswald and seeing his faith in God and knowing that 'by his faith he is speaking to us still' is the secret of life these days, and His sure knowledge that the best is yet to be. I feel as if it will be overwhelming to see what God has wrought one day."

For a time Mrs. Chambers, on her return to Britain, settled in Oxford. Kathleen, who was then a

small girl, recalls her mother typing away in the
basement, early and late, while at the same time
looking after three or four university students. "I
know this was a time when we had very little
money, and yet I don't ever remember any strain or
distress, only delight in doing God's will and being
absolutely sure that God would use *My Utmost*
mightily for His glory."

The task of gathering suitable extracts for that
wonderful book of daily readings, *My Utmost for
His Highest*, was a tremendous undertaking and involved much prayer and hard work. Through the
years it has proved to be a great blessing to multitudes of readers, and it has been translated into
quite a number of languages. The production of
this, along with some fifty other books, later produced what has been described as nothing short of
a miracle: "a worldwide library from nothing but
shorthand notes and a typewriter."[1]

Soon a group of intimate friends, some relatives
like Miss Gertrude Chambers and Miss Hobbs,
along with one or two businessmen who had known
Chambers in Egypt (or even in the days of the BTC),
gathered around Mrs. Chambers as an informal
committee with the purpose of forwarding the message of Oswald Chambers through the printed
page. Steadily the work went on; new books were
prepared and then printed as finances allowed.
Later there was formed the Oswald Chambers
Publications Association. The whole work was kept
free from commercialism, and advertising was

---

[1] Apart from the books published, the message of Chambers was
sent forth for twenty years (April 1932 to April 1952) in the publication of the *BTC Journal*, published monthly; most but not
all of the material used appeared later in book form.

rarely indulged in. The works of Chambers commended themselves to spiritual people, and one told another. Mrs. Chambers felt that it was her work to distribute the words of her husband in every way possible. She was especially anxious that missionaries and students should have the opportunity of sharing in the books. She never hesitated to give where there was a need, and hundreds of Bible students and missionary candidates received free copies and were encouraged to ask for more.

Meanwhile the steady sale of the books continued, and the account of their production and distribution as recorded in the minutes of the association is indeed a romance of God's working through dedicated lives who had no thought for themselves. There was, of course, much routine work behind the scenes, but it is interesting to note flashes of encouragement coming from time to time. Thus at one meeting there is a report of translation work in Dutch and German. Two years later, Swedish, Chinese, Japanese, and Braille were added to the list. Soon after, Spanish and Finnish and a suggestion of Arabic were included. For a long period there were no profits, but when there were these were put back into the production and distribution of more books.

Then came the war. Truly faith was tested. First problems of storage and of paper supplies, and then, most baffling of all, the destruction of the complete stock of thousands of books in the great fire of London (December 29–30, 1941). Yet there were notes of encouragement, as when the news came through that all the German stock of books were safe in Switzerland, and again news of translation into Hindi and Bengali. Just after the war a

Russian refugee wrote, very anxious to translate some of the books and leaflets into Russian. At the same time there were translations into Hungarian and Afrikaans.

It was noted that in the two years 1944–1945, a most difficult period, no less than 24,000 books were sold.

In the years since the war the good work has steadily continued. Most of the original helpers have passed on, but others equally devoted have taken their place. Kathleen Chambers, along with members of the council, maintains the standards expressed in the lives of her parents—standards of faith, loyalty to God's Word, and readiness for His leading for the future days.

Only a grain of wheat,
So small that folks don't mind it.
Only a grain of wheat,
With the power of God behind it.
There's a harvest in a grain of wheat,
If given to God in simple trust,
For though the grain doth turn to dust,
It cannot die, it lives; it must,
For the power of God is behind it.

—Anonymous

Appendix A:
Oswald Chambers: an
Evangelical Prophet[1]

Oswald Chambers left behind him no coherent and consistently worked out theological system. That is the last thing he would have desired. He would have claimed simply and with justice that his outlook was that of the Bible, so far as he understood it. He is, in fact, so thoroughly biblical that no literalist could find fault with his work, and yet he is so free that his intuitional exegesis frequently casts an entirely new light on familiar verses and fundamental doctrines. No man was such a student of the Bible; no man was more free from bibliolatry. His own Bible reading was constant and regular and his lifelong daily delight, yet he could prescribe for a seeker after a fuller life such a dose of other reading, especially in philosophy and psychology, that the inquirer's comment afterward was that the result was like a mental rebirth. There is a wonderful freshness in his Bible exposition that has been rare indeed in authentic evangelical circles in

---

[1]Reprinted by kind permission of the Bishop of Salisbury.

England during this century.

There is a moral grasp, too, of the inevitable tension of real Christian living, which can so easily be avoided by any shallow conception of holiness. Instead of the anemic separationism or the spineless worldliness of so much pseudo-evangelicalism, here is a deep insight into the depths of man's depravity. His emphasis on sin borders almost on dualism, with its reiterated refrain that "the basis of things is not rational, but tragic if it were rational; the Cross of Christ would be 'much ado about nothing'." And yet coupled with this goes sheer delight in all God's creatures and in all traces of His truth, goodness, and beauty, wherever these are found.

The artist in Oswald Chambers is swept away for a time after his initial conversion experiences, but comes back, the natural transformed into the spiritual by sacrifice. No one could accuse him of worldliness, yet no one was freer of the religious counterfeit of the life more abundant: which is no less a second-best following of the forerunner of the Lord rather than of the Lord himself, because among evangelicals it is called puritanism and not asceticism. There is a period at Dunoon when he scares congregations with his denunciations, but he passes to a fuller vision of the truth of God, which sees, as Evelyn Underhill puts it, that " 'the whole earth is full of his glory' means precisely what it says."

Over against such perverted evangelism of the Eliphaz type (Job 4:12), it is impressive to see in Oswald Chambers a man who experienced a most definite "second blessing" of sanctification, and yet passed on, not to deny the crucial importance of Luke 11:13[2]—a text that he kept on using in personal work—but to an ever greater faith in and reliance upon the inexhaustible riches of the person of our Lord regardless of all "varieties of religious experience," or lack of them. There is guidance for all evangelicals in this avoiding of both the Scylla of trust in "feelings" and also the Charybdis of self-deception in "kidding yourself" into believing that something has happened to you, simply because of some Bible text, when all the evidence is to the contrary—a tragic error that seems to be the evangelical counterpart of the Jesuit *excæcatio*. Between these two errors, or rather in alternating emphasis on each of them, lies the course of true progressive sanctification, marked in Chambers' case with an utter dependence upon God and yet issuing in a vitally active and not merely automatic passive obedience to the living Christ.

This, of course, meant for him a Christianity that was so thoroughly religious and divine that it could venture to be entirely secular and human. There is no need for the adoption of the defenses of clericalism or pseudo-piety of life or language. In his YMCA hut in Egypt, religion was so natural that it was really supernatural and capable of meeting the needs of those who were destined not for the cloisters but for the front-line trenches of Palestine. Nothing comes out more clearly in his final course of lectures on Ecclesiastes than his intense desire to bring Christ to the twentieth-century man of the world where he really was. Either salvation for a

---

[2]"If ye then, being evil, know how to give good gifts unto your children: how much more shall your heavenly Father give the Holy Spirit to them that ask him?"

soldier in Egypt was real at the front or it was a farce. This was no cultivation of hothouse mission plants.

Chambers' line of approach here seems to have been determined by his own personal experiences, though he never referred to them in his public talks, and castigates with devastating effect all who seek to build any work of God, either individual or corporate, upon "the reminiscent," i.e., upon the arguable and demonstrated basis of past evidence of God's favor and blessing. This to him is a denial of the fundamental reliance upon the Holy Spirit. It is to take the psychological approach to the soul and to substitute it for the pneumatic instead of using it as the invaluable instrument of the latter.

———

This brings us finally to his evangelism, first as a missionary, then at the Bible Training College, and finally in Egypt. Chambers did not stand still: there is no doubt that his views widened as his own insight deepened. It was always his greatest ambition to have "honorable mention" in anyone's relationship with Jesus Christ; but in the last year of his life he wrote "that the 'soul-saving passion' as an aim must cease and merge into the passion for Christ, revealing itself in holiness in all human relationships." This is written out of the abundant fruit of his personal work among the troops in Egypt. Here is a difference in emphasis from the great Holiness convention addresses of the middle period of his life, and perhaps a greater awareness of the infinite varieties of God's approach to the human soul.

———

Behind such teaching there was the glowing fire of a dominant and gifted personality, but Chambers did not use his gifts to lord over others in any domineering way. The freedom he allowed to those he cared for was coupled with intense, regular, persistent prayer for them. This twofold attitude would have led to an intolerable inner tension of spirit if it had not been the direct reflection of what he conceived to be God's attitude toward himself. God gave him complete freedom and yet in every detail of daily life unceasingly cared for him. He reflected his Master's voice. Again and again he reverts to the sparrows and the lilies, and in the spirit of Matthew 6:25 he comes out with the emphatic "I *refuse* to worry." This is what kept his own spirit so childlike and boyish in all his dealings with the troops in Egypt and with his own daughter, while at the same time leaving him quite free from the all too frequent stigma of arrested development and failure to grow up into mature adult life.

———

It is the great service of Oswald Chambers to have recalled evangelicals to that dangerous creative living, which, being on the yonder side of convention, is always a stumbling block to traditional orthodoxy, whether parental or ecclesiastical. In his writings and in his life is shown a wonderful grasp of both sides of the frequent dilemmas of Christian faith and conduct. He gloried in Emerson's remark that "consistency is the hobgoblin of little minds," and this in no sense of Gnostic superiority, but out of the conviction that only in the paradoxes of seeming antitheses can the full range of Christian truth and living be grasped by the mind and in the experience of man.

Best of all, through his writings there is a real opening up of the springs of biblical life, which convention and tradition—evangelical quite as much as Catholic—continually seal up. To drink at the living waters of Chambers' work is to receive new inspiration to dig again the wells of life for oneself. Only in so doing shall we rediscover the glorious freedom and freshness of that revival of true religion that we so desperately need and which has nothing in common with the pseudo-spirituality that Chambers simply could not stand. On his tombstone in Old Cairo is inscribed simply the epitaph "A believer in Jesus Christ": no frills, no fancies, but a life that "being dead, yet speaketh" and confronts us all at all times, and especially in our Bible reading, with the glorious expectancy of its ringing challenge: "In my study am I a woolgatherer or like a man looking for his Lord?" (J. E. Fison, C.F.)

Appendix B:
On Reading Oswald Chambers

For those approaching the books of Oswald Chambers and seeking some guidance, we give the following suggestions:

1. Remember the setting: they are from verbatim notes of lectures and sermons reproduced just as they were given.

2. Read with the Bible at hand, looking up all references.

3. Read other helpful books alongside: e.g., *Studies in the Sermon on the Mount* might be well supplemented with Bishop Gore's book (warmly commended by Chambers) and Stanley Jones' *Christ of the Mount*.

4. Do not read too much at a time. Chambers' message is so concentrated that it is best taken in small doses.

5. Use *My Utmost for His Highest* for daily reading; it provides a continual link with the style and message of Chambers.

The following outline may be helpful as it summarizes the main themes and cites the works appropriate to each.

A. The Need for Reality (orthodoxy not enough)
   Facing Reality
   Baffled to Fight Better
   Shade of His Hand
B. The Basis of Redemption (life's foundations redemptive, not rational)
   Shadow of an Agony
   Psychology of Redemption
   Bringing Sons to Glory
C. The Experience in Christian Life (true holiness, Christ's life in us)
   Our Brilliant Heritage
   Studies in the Sermon on the Mount
   If Ye Shall Ask (the prayer life)
D. The Expression in Service
   Not Knowing Whither (the call and guidance)
   So Send I You (as above, with missionary emphasis)
   Workmen of God
   Approved Unto God

The above does not cover all. There are strands of teaching beyond, especially those along the lines of Christian psychology and biblical ethics (e.g., *The Philosophy of Sin, Moral Foundations of Life*, and *If Thou Wilt Be Perfect*).

Appendix C:
Notes on the Writings of
Oswald Chambers

(Listed in order of publication, as far as can be ascertained.)

The Discipline of Suffering
The Discipline of Loneliness
The Discipline of Guidance
These three booklets, based on talks given in America before the war, were first issued by the Cincinnati Bible School. More recently they have appeared as two volumes called *Christian Discipline*. These, unlike the later books, bear the marks of having been edited by Chambers; one feature is the prolific use of apt poetic quotations.

Studies in the Sermon on the Mount
This small volume first appeared in America, being made up of Bible studies at the Cincinnati Bible School. It was later published in Great Britain, and has remained a favorite among Chambers' writings.

Biblical Psychology

Based on lectures at the BTC in 1912, used later in the YMCA classes at Zeitoun. The closing words are significant:

> This ends abruptly, but we leave it so. The whole book is merely a verbatim report of the lectures, and we have decided to let it go for what it is worth—a mere effort to rouse up the average Christian worker to study the wealth of the Scriptures and to become better equipped for dividing the Word of truth.

This is a book not for devotional reading but for systematic study. The emphasis is essentially biblical in nature, and the whole can only be appreciated by those who accept the revelation truths concerning man, conveyed through the Scriptures.

My Utmost for His Highest

The most popular and widely used of all. A book of daily readings, now a spiritual classic in worldwide demand. It has been translated into at least twelve languages, including Chinese and Arabic. When Brother Douglas presented a specially bound copy to the late Queen Mary, in the letter of thanks from her Lady in Waiting there came these words:

> Various people at different times have sent the Queen books of daily reading but this one seems quite different from the ordinary, more stereotyped variety, and I think Her Majesty will read it with real interest and, I hope, comfort.

To quote Mrs. Chambers in her foreword:

> A large proportion of the readings have been

chosen from the talks given during the devotional hour at the college—an hour that marked for so many of the students an epoch in their life with God. "Men return again and again to the few who have mastered the spiritual secret, whose life has been hid with Christ in God. These are of the old-time religion, hung to the nails of the cross" (Robert Murray McCheyne). It is because it is felt that the author is one to whose teaching men will return, that this book has been prepared, and it is sent out with the prayer that day by day the messages may continue to bring the quickening life and inspiration of the Holy Spirit.

Jim Reimann has recently updated the language of this book to reflect modern-day English usage. This invaluable service has made this classic accessible to an even greater number of people.

Baffled to Fight Better

These remarkable studies in the Book of Job, and some of the pressing problems it stirs up, were given to the troops in Egypt. The first edition, printed in very simple form mainly for those in active service, appeared in December 1917, just after the home call of the author. A number of later editions have succeeded through the years and the appeal remains as strong as ever. It is a book for those facing the problem of life's sufferings and tragedies. Two notes of warning: (1) Do not be disturbed by the rugged direct language used—remember Chambers was speaking to men facing the horrors of war. (2) Do not let the alliteration of the headings be a barrier. They appeared first on a blackboard, and no doubt arrested attention.

The Place of Help

This is a book of devotional readings, but not arranged for daily use as is *My Utmost*. It is made up of undated sermons preached in Britain for the most part, of devotional talks given at the Bible Training College, and of messages at Sunday services in Egypt.

Of the last, someone who heard them wrote:

> The sermons at Zeitoun in those years of strain and stress were the very sacrament of preaching: no one could doubt it who heard with the keen hearing of the spiritual ear the miracle of authentic stillness that falls upon an assembly of men in those rare moments when a man speaks to his hearers, spirit to spirit, and he and they alike know it. The moment passes, but the "inward and spiritual grace" abides—a sacramental permanent possession.

It is worth noting the tides of the last messages given before the end: "The Deep Embarrassments of God" (Hosea 11); "Getting Into God's Stride" (Genesis 5:24); and finally, "Disabling Shadows of the Soul" (Ecclesiastes 12:5).

We especially commend this book for devotional reading—it contains no less than forty messages.

Shade of His Hand

This book contains the very last lectures delivered at Zeitoun on Ecclesiates: the last chapter is missing, as chapter 12 was never expounded. Like the studies in Job, *Shade of His Hand* deals with life in the raw. It is a study in the reactions of human nature to all that life brings. There is an anticipation of many of the problems facing young people today. The only answer to the question "Is life worth living?" is to be found in the reality of Christ who redeems life from all its vanity.

The Shadow of an Agony

This book, made up of talks given in Egypt, was published just after the war, and its first edition had a striking introduction by P. T. Forsyth, who wrote of this book: "The writer has no 'pi-talk' [pious talk], nor is he but a rouser. Not only is his manner direct and searching but he has a real educated grasp of the moral nature of the spiritual soul and its psychology. He has a happy combination of the familiar style and the competent stuff. His is the kind of address of which we have too little—the union of moral incision and spiritual power. I am glad to commend such teaching, and I hope the stringency of the times will develop more preachers who have this gift—not of talking about the spiritual life but of penetrating the conscience of it with some moral psychology in the name of a positive gospel. It is the kind of evangelism we deeply need, the sound modernizing of redemption. We are too familiar with ways of bringing peace to a man's mind that are not true to the fundament of things."

Psychology of Redemption

This is a study in the Christian life as running parallel with the life of our Lord. "His Birth and Our New Birth," "His Baptism and Our Vocation," and so on to the climax of "His Ascension and Our Union." This was a line of teaching that Chambers used continually, illustrating the sanctified life from the life of our Lord set forth in the Gospels. Its teaching has been compared to that of Henry Scougal's *Life of God in the Soul of Man*, a volume that greatly influenced Whitfield and the Wesleys. Scougal wrote:

> The power and life of religion may be better expressed in actions than in words. . . . They are perfectly exemplified in the holy life of our blessed Savior, a main part of whose business in this world was to teach by His practice what He did require of others; and to make His own conversation an exact resemblance of those rules that He prescribed.

So Send I You

This is a book for candidates for the mission field, but not for them alone. As the late Dr. Zwemer says in a foreword:

> The twenty-two short chapters are in a sense Bible studies, but they are not mere Bible readings of texts with a moral. They whisper the secret of the burning heart, of the fully surrendered life, of a love that will not let go. The words pulsate with life and are a clarion-call away from idle daydreams to the stern path of duty.

The opening chapters dealing with "The Call" are particularly useful.

Not Knowing Whither

This is a series of studies in the life of Abraham. In a sense it is also a handbook for those hearing the call into Christ's service. The emphasis is on the way of faith, which is always the way of trust and obedience. It is a remarkable character study in the outstanding figure in Genesis; nowhere else, in our judgment, does Chambers reach such heights of effective exposition.

Workmen of God

This powerful and searching book (originally published as the *Discipline of Souls*) expresses the experience gained by Oswald Chambers in dealing with individuals. It is not a shallow worker's handbook giving suitable texts for various cases. The treatment goes much deeper. The true worker of God must first of all be familiar with the revelation facts in God's book; then he must know people, and finally and most of all he must be in close touch with God, himself relying upon the Holy Spirit to bring back the right word at the right time.

The various types to be met with are classified in an original way. There are first the abnormal, all who are apart from God; then the hardy annuals, healthy-minded sinners illustrated by three New Testament pagans—Galleo, the indifferent; Herod, the hardened; and Pilate, the compromiser. Then there are the backsliders and the two-faced (hypocrites). Another class is described as the sick souls, and finally the stupid, that is, the morally obstinate.

The true worker must have a passion for souls and a shepherd's heart. Here Chambers brings in a personal note from his early days:

I did not like it at the time but I am thankful now I had to do shepherding in the Highlands of Scotland. When you have to carry across your shoulders a dirty old wether and bring it down the mountainside, you will soon know whether it is not the most taxing, the most exhausting, and the most exasperating work; and Jesus uses this as an illustration of a passion for souls.

Christ wants us to be broken bread and poured

out wine, that others may be saved.

In order to catch men for the Lord Jesus Christ
you must love Him beyond all others; you must
have a consuming passion of love, then He will
flow through you in love and yearning and draw
men to himself.

The final note is an insistence on spiritual concentration to prove oneself "a workman that
needeth not to be ashamed" (2 Timothy 2:15).

The Moral Foundations of Life

These studies deal with the ethics of the Christian life and its psychology. Chapters headed:
"Habit," "Behavior," "Direction of the Will," "What
to Think About," are full of practical, down-to-earth
guidance for the day-by-day living of the Christian
life.

The Philosophy of Sin

This also deals with the practical, moral problems that every man must face, no less the Christian than the pagan. The emphasis on sin is set
against the reality of redemption. "If sin is a radical
twist with a supernatural originator, salvation is a
radical adjustment with a supernatural Originator. . . . It is only the right view of sin and right
thinking about sin that ever will explain Jesus
Christ's life and death and resurrection."

If Thou Wilt Be Perfect

Chambers had evidently been reading the mystics, and out of that came these remarkable studies.
Tauler, who lived in the 1300s and was a great
preacher, had a remarkable experience (we wonder
if Chambers saw in this a shadow of his own). An

unknown layman who heard him preach, told him that he was being "killed by the letter" and was yet in darkness. Tauler took these words meekly and for a time ceased from preaching, living humbly a life of contemplation, seeking God's way. His friends thought he was mad. However, the light dawned and he knew the time had come for him to preach again, which he did with great spiritual effect. His sermons were published under the title *The Following of Christ*. Then there was the *Theologia Germanica*, another mystic book by an unknown writer, stressing the work of the Holy Spirit in applying Christ to the believing heart. Quotations from these two unusual sources are scattered throughout these chapters, but the teaching is well anchored in Scripture. The whole effect is to make dear the depth and reality of Christian perfection. It is well summed up in the sentence, "The devotion to Jesus Christ of our person is the effectual working of the evangelical doctrine of Christian perfection." This is definitely a book for those who are spiritually mature.

If Ye Shall Ask

These studies in the prayer life are quite unique even as was their writer. The opening chapter, "What's the Good of Prayer?" given originally to the troops in Egypt, brings home the reality of real prayer, prayer that changes us and through us changes things. Chambers himself lived such a life of intercession for others that he could not but speak with authority on the power of prayer based on redemption. Behind all effective prayer is a simple relationship with Jesus Christ.

Bringing Sons to Glory

These studies follow the same line as the *Psychology of Redemption*. Our Lord's life and the great points of crisis in it are taken as reflecting something in the spiritual life of the believer. The theology of Christ's person, both human and divine, is treated very fully. The *kenosis* and the *plerosis*, the self-emptying and the fulfillment of Christ, are set forth in a striking and helpful way. The main emphasis, however, is on the possibility of that union with Christ that is the inheritance of every real believer.

Biblical Ethics

This is definitely a study book but, as ever, with a practical spiritual end in view. The problems of human conduct both individually and socially are dwelt upon. The section headed "Spiritual Construction" is most helpful as is the latter section, "With Christ in the School of Philosophy" (how to think about God, about man, about sin, about the Scriptures, etc.).

He Shall Glorify Me

Mainly concerned with understanding the work of the Holy Spirit, this book was compiled primarily from messages given to the men in Egypt and later printed as leaflets. These studies are of individual value apart from the main subject matter.

Conformed to His Image

In this selection there is a psychological emphasis. Christian thinking occupies almost half the book, followed by studies in the psychology of faith. It must always be remembered that Chambers taught before the days of the so-called "New Psychology" (Freud, Jung, etc.). For him, psychology was the use of the mind in strenuous and disciplined thinking, and it was essential that we "think as Christians."

God's Workmanship

This more recently published volume (1953) consists of some thirty messages, given at different times and in diverse places to many sorts and conditions of men. Such titles as "Don't Think Now, Take the Road," "Spasmodic Spiritually," "Enchanted but Unchanged," suggest something of the wealth of spiritual teaching handed out so lavishly.

Approved Unto God

This, again, is a book for the worker. The emphasis is on the spiritually disciplined life of the true worker for God. A man of God must be thoroughly furnished unto every good work. It is a challenge to disciplined preparation for God's service. The latter part of the book is "Facing Reality," a very practical study, which we would commend to any concerned with the reality behind the creeds and doctrines of the faith. Just the book for a young budding agnostic.

The Servant As His Lord

A recent compilation of earlier booklets. *The Fighting Chance*, stressing the strenuous side of the Christian life; *The Soul of a Christian*, dealing with the inner life of the saint; *The Sacrament of Saints*, a moving study of the experience whereby dedicated souls may become broken bread on which others can feast.

Our Portrait in Genesis

Brief studies in the early chapters of Genesis. "There are flashes of light on God's relation to fallen man that can touch a live nerve in a modern wrong-doer; and something of the divine mercy is seen as it persists with perverse and misguided men."

Knocking at God's Door

This selection of prayers not meant for any other eye, reveals a saint in familiar communion with his Father. To use these prayers and enter into something of their meaning and spirit cannot but make us better men and women of Christ.

Disciples Indeed

A different volume from all that has gone before. It is made up of sentences, *obiter dicta*, from the lecture hall and the pulpit, arranged under headings. Those under "Study," "Preparation," and "Thinking" are very meaty and challenging: e.g., "More danger arises from physical laziness than from almost any other thing. Beware of saying, 'I haven't time to read the Bible or to pray'; say rather, 'I haven't disciplined myself to do these things.'"

Booklets—later published in book form

Our Brilliant Heritage

The subtitle "Gospel Mystery of Sanctification," suggests the Puritan Walter Marshall, who wrote under that title. The teaching is that sanctification means:

The impartation to us and through us of the Lord Jesus Christ, His patience, His purity, His holiness. Not that Jesus Christ enables us to imitate Him, not that the power of God is in us and we try our best and fail, and try again, but that the very virtues of Jesus Christ are manifested in our mortal flesh.

Grow Up Into Him

Here we have very practical studies in Christian living, the teaching revolving around the place of habit in the spiritual life. God regenerates us and puts us in touch with His divine resources, but He cannot make us walk in His way; the practicing is ours, not God's.

As He Walked

This follows the same line as the above, the emphasis being on the living out of the Christ-life, not by imitation but by expressing the Christ-life imparted to us in the gift of the Spirit.

The Highest Good

This is a study of Christian ethics. We note the quotations from James Stalker's *The Ethic of Jesus*. Again the impression given is that the teaching of Jesus demanded more than that of the scribes and Pharisees. It is not our acts but our motives that matter most.

The Great Redemption

As the title indicates, this is a study in redemption as it comes to us through the revelation of Jesus Christ; not so much a plan of salvation, but a redeeming Person.

The Pilgrim's Song Book

Here we have devotional studies in Psalms 120 to 128, the songs of the pilgrims going up to Zion. From these as from all Scripture, Chambers draws many practical and challenging lessons.

The Love of God
Expresses the worldwide yet personal love of God, how it is "shed abroad in our hearts," and the difference it makes.

For Further Reading

For further study into the life of Oswald Chambers, we heartily recommend that you read *Oswald Chambers: Abandoned to God*, by David McCasland. Published by Discovery House Publishers in 1993, it was the recipient of the Gold Medallion Book Award given by the Evangelical Christian Publishers Association. This 350-page volume is the definitive work on the life and times of Oswald Chambers. Included are sixty poems from his pen and sixty-two photographs from his life. Eugene Peterson, the James M. Houston Professor of Spiritual Theology at Regent College and the author of *The Message*, wrote, "So many millions of us have read his words—been deepened by his prayers, been brought before God by his writing. And now we get to know him. I had no idea what a magnificent life was present behind these marvelous words. Oswald Chambers' writing is validated in detail after detail by his life."

INTRODUCE YOURSELF TO ANOTHER HERO OF THE FAITH.

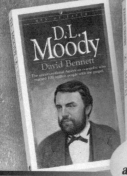

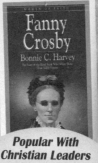

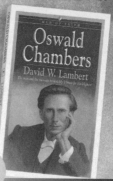

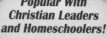

Popular With Christian Leaders and Homeschoolers!

Gathered from across centuries and continents, the biographies in the MEN and WOMEN OF FAITH series all have one thing in common—an inspiring example of a person dedicated to living fully for God. Whether missionary, writer, theologian, or ordinary citizen, each person featured in the series provides us with both encouragement for our own lives as well as an appreciation of our spiritual history.

Often thrilling and always compelling, the MEN and WOMEN OF FAITH biographies ensure that the stories of our Christian heritage will continue to live on.

Thank you for selecting a book from
BETHANY HOUSE PUBLISHERS

Bethany House Publishers is a ministry of Bethany
Fellowship International, an interdenominational,
nonprofit organization committed to spreading the
Good News of Jesus Christ around the world through
evangelism, church planting, literature distribution,
and care for those in need. Missionary training is
offered through Bethany College of Missions.

Bethany Fellowship International is a member of the
National Association of Evangelicals and subscribes to
its statement of faith. If you would like further
information, please contact:

Bethany Fellowship International
6820 Auto Club Road
Minneapolis, MN 55438 USA